THE HAIKU ANTHOLOGY

THE
HAIKU
ANTHOLOGY

Haiku and Senryu in English

Edited by Cor van den Heuvel

W. W. Norton & Company New York London

The text of this book is composed in Stempel Garamond
with the display set in Weiss.
Composition by Chelsea Dippel
Manufacturing by the Maple-Vail Book Manufacturing Group
Book design by Chris Welch

Library of Congress Cataloging-in-Publication Data

The haiku anthology : haiku and senryu in English / edited by
Cor van den Heuvel. — [3rd ed.]

p.   cm.

Includes bibliographical references (p.   ).

ISBN 0-393-04743-1

1. Haiku, American. 2. Haiku, Canadian. 3. Senryu, American. 4. Senryu,
Canadian. 5. Nature—Poetry.   I. Van den Heuvel, Cor, 1931–   .
PS593.H3H34   1999
811'.04108—dc21   98-50927
CIP

ISBN 0-393-32118-5 pbk.

W. W. Norton & Company, Inc.
500 Fifth Avenue, New York, N.Y. 10110
www.wwnorton.com

W. W. Norton & Company Ltd.
Castle House, 75/76 Wells Street, London W1T 3QT

4 5 6 7 8 9 0

To Harold G. Henderson and R. H. Blyth

I would like to thank the poets for their help in putting together this book, particularly Carl Patrick for his critical advice and L. A. Davidson for the use of her library of haiku books and magazines. I'd also like to express my appreciation to Gerald Howard, who was my first editor at Norton, for suggesting I do a third edition, and to Norton editor Patricia Chui for guiding it through the publishing process.

A special thanks to my wife, Leonia Leigh Larrecq van den Heuvel, for her love and support through three editions of *The Haiku Anthology*.

CONTENTS

A NOTE ON THE
SELECTION AND LAYOUT
OF THE POEMS

Selection: Some readers may wonder why I've chosen certain poems in this book which are, on the surface, similar to others. If a haiku is a good one, it doesn't matter if the subject has been used before. The writing of variations on certain subjects in haiku, sometimes using the same or similar phrases (or even changing a few words of a previous haiku), is one of the most interesting challenges the genre offers a poet and can result in refreshingly different ways of "seeing anew" for the reader. This is an aspect of traditional Japanese haiku which is hard for many Westerners, with their ideas of uniqueness and Romantic individualism, to accept. But some of the most original voices in haiku do not hesitate to dare seeming derivative if they see a way of reworking an "old" image.

Layout: Due to the fact that the words of a haiku provide only the bare essentials of the image, with which the reader's awareness works to create the haiku moment, it is important that the reader is not distracted from those essentials. The layout of the page, the amount of white space within which the words may work, and the choice of the other haiku on the spread all play a role in determining how the reader will direct his or her attention. Such considerations have been second only to the selection of the haiku themselves in the editing of this book.

Haiku. What is it about these small poems that makes people all over the world want to read and write them? Nick Virgilio, one of America's first major haiku poets, once said in an interview that he wrote haiku "to get in touch with the real." And the Haiku Society of America has called haiku a "poem in which Nature is linked to human nature." We all want to know what is real and to feel at one with the natural world. Haiku help us to experience the everyday things around us vividly and directly, so we see them as they really are, as bright and fresh as they were when we first saw them as children. Haiku is basically about living with intense awareness, about having an openness to the existence around us—a kind of openness that involves seeing, hearing, smelling, tasting, and touching.

Not so long ago, in 1991, when the first Haiku North America conference was being held at Las Positas College outside of San Francisco, another major figure of American haiku, J. W. Hackett, and his wife, Pat, invited four of the attending poets including myself to their garden home on a hill in the Santa Cruz mountains. Christopher Herold, one of those poets, wrote a haiku, included in this anthology, about that experience:

> returning quail
> call to us from the moment
> of which he speaks

The poets had all moved out to the garden, continuing their talk about nature, Zen, and haiku. Toasts were raised to Bashō, Japan's most famous haiku poet, and to R. H. Blyth, his most faithful translator. Shadows were lengthening and James Hackett was trying to make clear his feelings about haiku when the birds suddenly came to his assistance. Christopher Herold's haiku captures that "moment" of the afternoon, when Hackett, and the quail, summed up everything he had been saying, eloquently and passionately, about haiku and the way of life it represents: living in the present moment—now.

That conference the poets were attending is just one indication of the new popularity of haiku. The Haiku North America conferences bring together poets from many different haiku groups and societies throughout the United States and Canada. They are held every other year. The first two were at Las Positas, the third was in Toronto, and in 1997 the conference was held at Portland State University, in Portland, Oregon. The next one is scheduled for Chicago. There have recently been a number of international conferences as well. There was one in Matsuyama in 1990, with delegates from the United States, China, and several European countries meeting with some of the top haiku poets and critics of Japan. In Chicago in 1995 about twenty Japanese haiku poets came to join American and Canadian haiku poets in a series of events called Haiku Chicago, which included a haiku-writing walk through Chicago streets and parks.

There have been others: in Europe, California, and one just last year in Tokyo, which was hosted by the Haiku International Association and attended by a large delegation from the Haiku Society of America and Haiku Canada. These larger activities are the result of smaller groups of haiku poets getting together in their own individual countries to write haiku, to publish magazines and books on the subject, and to discuss haiku theory and practice. This phenomenon is nowhere more prevalent than in the

United States, which probably has more poets writing haiku than any other country except Japan. Groups of poets have joined together in Boston, New York, Chicago, Washington, D.C., Portland, Oregon, San Francisco, and many other cities and towns across America to write and discuss haiku. The Haiku Society of America has helped to coordinate and organize special events, such as the conferences mentioned above, to bring these groups together for an interchange of ideas and mutual encouragement. Many of the groups were started within the society's regional division program, which allows each region to elect its own regional director, have regional meetings, and have its own newsletter or magazine. Many of the poets in this anthology have been active in such groups.

Despite such serious attempts to develop a haiku literature, and to educate the public about it, there is still a lot of misunderstanding about this kind of poetry. The idea that haiku is anything in three lines of 5-7-5 syllables dies hard. People write little epigrams in this form, or jokes about Spam, or cute descriptions of birds and flowers, and think they are writing haiku.

In 1987, I wrote in *The New York Times Book Review*:

A haiku is *not* just a pretty picture in three lines of 5-7-5 syllables each. In fact, most haiku in English are not written in 5-7-5 syllables at all—many are not even written in three lines. What distinguishes a haiku is concision, perception and awareness—not a set number of syllables. A haiku is a short poem recording the essence of a moment keenly perceived in which Nature is linked to human nature. As Roland Barthes has pointed out, this record neither describes nor defines, but "diminishes to the point of pure and sole designation." The poem is refined into a touchstone of suggestiveness. In the mind of an aware reader it opens again into an image that is immediate and palpable, and pulsing with that delight of the senses that carries a conviction of one's unity with all of existence. A haiku can be anywhere from a few to 17 syllables, rarely more. It is now known that about 12—not 17—syllables in English are equivalent in length to the 17 *onji* (sound-symbols) of the Japanese haiku. A number of poets are writing them shorter than that. The results almost literally fit Alan Watts's description of haiku as "wordless" poems. Such poems may seem flat and empty to the uninitiated. But despite their simplicity, haiku can be very demanding of both writer and reader, being at the same time one of the most accessible and inaccessible kinds of poetry. R. H. Blyth, the great translator of Japanese haiku, wrote that a haiku is "an open door which looks shut." To see what is suggested by a haiku, the reader must share in the creative process, being willing to associate and pick up on the echoes implicit in the words. A wrong focus, or lack of awareness, and he will see only a closed door.

At the time I wrote that article the activities of the Haiku Society of America were pretty much confined to New York City, though it had members throughout the country, and most of the small groups mentioned above were yet to be formed. Soon after this the HSA began to hold its annual meeting in a different city each year, and the regional system was created. All the special conferences mentioned above have taken place in the decade of the nineties. The world of English-language haiku has radically changed since the last edition of this book in 1986.

At the same time as these developments were taking place, haiku's sister genre, senryu, was also increasing in popularity and in quality. Senryu is the same as haiku except, instead of dealing with Nature, it is specifically about human nature and human relationships and is often humorous. Many poets writing haiku in English also write senryu. For many Americans writing them, senryu is haiku—though a very special kind. But as many others consider them totally different genres, without disputing that they have the same roots and retain many similarities. They both embody an awareness of the world around us.

Besides the wider developments discussed above, yet partly due to them, the more important goals of creating excellent haiku and producing individual writers of talent continue to be realized. New, young poets have come to the fore. Established poets have broadened and deepened their work. New haiku magazines and presses have appeared. And new books of haiku and about haiku have significantly altered the way we think about the genre. (See the Book List following this foreword, where magazines and organizations are also listed.)

In this book there are about 850 haiku and senryu by eighty-nine poets. Around half of the poems are new to this edition. Forty-four of the poets appear in the anthology for the first time. I will get to a brief discussion of some of these new writers shortly. But poets have been writing haiku in North America since at least the 1950s, and I would like to first say something about the early figures of English-language haiku, for their work is included here as well.

Two major poets from this group have died since the last edition of this book appeared. The loss to haiku by the deaths of Nicholas Virgilio and John Wills is immeasurable. Both were respected in the American haiku world from their earliest appearances in the little magazines. By the time of their deaths they were considered among the top writers of the genre. Since their passing their stature has become even more assured. Their works stand as monuments on the landscape of American haiku's first half century. That period, beginning in the fifties and early sixties with the first experiments of Jack Kerouac, J. W. Hackett, Nick Virgilio, and others, and which is now being crowned with the mature works of a number of outstanding haiku poets, may someday be looked upon as the Golden Age of North American Haiku.

Nick Virgilio died at age sixty in January of 1989. He was stricken by a heart attack while taping an interview for *The Charlie Rose Show,* a nationally televised program then airing on CBS. Nick had been a popular figure as a guest on television and radio in the Philadelphia area, interesting thousands of people in haiku. During the year or so before his death, he appeared a number of times on National Public Radio. When he died, he was on the verge of becoming American haiku's first celebrity. Virgilio's work is far-ranging, from simple nature poems to gritty urban haiku. His haiku about his brother, who died in Vietnam, comprise one of the finest elegies ever written. They demonstrate the power of love to preserve the memory of those close to us.

Through the Nick Virgilio Haiku Association, headquartered in his hometown of Camden, New Jersey, Nick still spreads the word about haiku. He is buried there only a few steps from Walt Whitman's tomb. Whitman was one of his favorite poets, and Nick often quoted him. A large granite stone in the shape of a lectern has been erected over Nick's grave with his famous "lily" haiku engraved on its top. Visitors can read the poem while facing a small lily pond:

> lily:
> out of the water . . .
> out of itself

John Wills died in 1993 at the age of seventy-two. His haiku go deep into the heart of American nature. Many of his greatest haiku were written between 1971 and 1978 when he lived on a farm in the mountains of Tennessee. They are about the surrounding fields and woods and the streams and rivers. He loved fishing and wrote often about it in his haiku. With just the barest of brushstrokes, Wills can make us one with a waterthrush at dusk or let us see the miracle that lies in a simple swirl of water on a trout stream:

> rain in gusts
> below the deadhead
> troutswirl

Happily, one of American haiku's most important pioneering writers, J. W. Hackett, is still with us, and we can, as I noted earlier, drink a toast to Bashō with him. Hackett's haiku first appeared in the early sixties. R. H. Blyth included a selection as an appendix to his *History of Haiku* in 1964. He cited Hackett's works as examples of how haiku could be written in English. In 1986, I wrote in the preface to the Second Edition of this book that Hackett had turned to writing longer works. But in the nineties he has begun writing haiku again and has become active in the haiku community. He recently lectured about haiku in Japan, Ireland, and the United States and has judged several haiku contests, including the annual contest of the British Haiku Society. In 1993 he was the keynote speaker at the second Haiku North America. He is finishing a new book about haiku to be called *That Art Thou: My Way of Haiku*. Hackett's haiku included here are from his popular *The Zen Haiku and Other Zen Poems of J. W. Hackett,* which is still in print (see the Book List for this and for a Web site devoted to his work).

Among the other important trailblazers of English-language haiku included in this edition are Clement Hoyt, who started studying haiku and Zen with Nyogen Senzaki in 1936 and became one of our first senryu writers; O. Mabson Southard, who has described his poetic voice as owing "the burden of its intimate heraldry to aboriginal America"; Robert Spiess, many of whose haiku reflect his love of canoeing the lakes and streams of Wisconsin; Elizabeth Searle Lamb, who has traveled widely, but writes some of her best haiku about the American Southwest, where she now lives; L. A. Davidson, a sharp observer of nature as it exists in New York City, where she has long resided, and whose love of sailing probably played a part in the creation of her well-known "beyond / stars" haiku; Foster Jewell, who captured the silences of the woods and desert places of America; and Eric Amann, a Canadian poet, critic, and editor, who is able to find haiku in parking lots and on billboards, and even in a folded tent:

> The circus tent
> all folded up:
> October mist . . .

The haiku of all of these poets began appearing in the early haiku magazines of the sixties. Some of those poets edited these magazines. Hoyt and Spiess were both early editors of the first haiku magazine in this country, *American Haiku*. The first issue, published in 1963, contained work by Hackett, Virgilio, and Southard. Spiess has for many years now been the editor of *Modern Haiku*, and Lamb was for a long time the editor of *Frogpond*, the magazine of the Haiku Society of America. Eric Amann started the first Canadian haiku magazine, *Haiku*, in 1967. Hoyt and Jewell passed away some time ago. Of the rest, only Spiess, Lamb, and Davidson have been notably active in recent years, writing and publishing new haiku.

As English-language haiku approaches the end of its first fifty years, a number of poets, other than those discussed already, have, by the quality and quantity of their haiku, emerged as major figures: Anita Virgil, Gary Hotham, Marlene Mountain, Alexis Rotella, George Swede, Alan Pizzarelli, Michael McClintock, Raymond Roseliep, and Rod Willmot.

Roseliep, who died in 1983, was one of our most unorthodox poets. He used haiku in an intellectual, yet paradoxical, and spiritual, way. At the same time he saw the world as vividly sensuous and richly comical. The play of the mind is usually avoided in American haiku, yet Roseliep was successful in using it because he did so so innovatively, and because he infused it with the haiku spirit. Michael McClintock, another major revolutionary in haiku, has not been noticeably active for some time now—though he quietly published a book in 1997 that may contain haiku (see Biographical Notes). His early defense of a "liberated haiku" and his critical rejection of syllable counting were crucial in the development of English-language haiku. His senryu magazine *seer ox* was instrumental in gaining respect for senryu at a time, the mid-seventies, when not a few haiku poets looked down on it. His work here is taken from that included in the Second Edition. Rod Willmot, another original, helped change haiku's direction by his critical articles and by his broken-narrative style of haiku. He has also not been heard much in haiku circles recently. However, he did publish quite a bit in the years immediately following the last edition, and I've included a number of these newer pieces. His Burnt Lake Press was important in the late eighties and published, with Black Moss, Virgilio's and Wills's most important books. He is now at work on a novel.

Gary Hotham is a haiku poet whose work is continually exciting. He keeps turning out wonderfully subtle and simple poems, honing them to a pitch of perfection until they quietly consecrate the quotidian. Some of his newer works create a noir-like atmosphere. In just a few words, he can convey a feeling of small-town loneliness, the bleakness at the edges of a big city, or the mystery and wonder at the heart of the most ordinary happenings of a life in the suburbs.

Though I've included several new pieces by Marlene Mountain, most of her section contains earlier haiku. For about a decade now she has concentrated on what she herself has characterized as "pissed off poems." These are works that express her outrage at what we have done and are doing to harm the environment and to limit the freedom of women. To me, most of these seem, however admirable, something other than haiku or senryu. Her "belly up" frog and a few others may be exceptions.

Since the Second Edition, Anita Virgil has added significantly to her already impressive body of work, writing haiku that give us the essence of our American seasons and senryu that zero in on the human condition. She is also one of our best haibun (a mixed form of prose and haiku) writers, combining a lucid, supple prose with haiku that grow out of it as easily as flowers, or cucumbers, from a vine. She notices with keen awareness things around her that many of us take for granted or fail to observe at all. There is a lot of her new work included here.

George Swede and Alexis Rotella are beyond superlatives. They are both masters of haiku and senryu, and you will find an abundance of new as well as time-tested work by them in this edition. Alexis Rotella's poetry reflects the wide spectrum of existence itself, aglow with the special light of art. Her senryu contain vivid exposures of her personal life. Rod Willmot said of her work: "Although [Rotella] has a wide range, her special gift is for the revelation of moments in her emotional relationships with others . . . She catches the most troublesome of such material and puts it down *perfectly*, without a trace of pretence or self-indulgence, capturing it so simply and accurately that henceforth that moment of human experience, in anyone's life, is expressed for all time."

George Swede is the funniest haiku poet who ever lived. I'm sure his senryu would be the envy of great comedy writers like Woody Allen or Mel Brooks if they were aware of them. The opening and closing lines of his section in this book are priceless. He teaches the Psychology of Art and Creativity at Ryerson Polytechnic University in Toronto and has been a featured speaker at many of the HNA and international conferences mentioned above.

Alan Pizzarelli is one of this book's biggest attractions. It's too bad I can't hang a circus banner from the cover saying, "Don't Miss the Greatest Haiku Act on Earth!" Since the Second Edition, his work has reached a level of quality that fills me with joy and envy. Pizzarelli finds his subject matter everywhere: in a piece of burlap, on a car bumper, or in the actions of a shoeshine boy. With a special kind of insight, he is able to spot the moment that shows their significance and is able to reveal it through an extraordinary facility with words.

Of the other poets here that have been in earlier editions, Arizona Zipper is one of several who have made notable strides in their work, and he has a much larger selection this time. His haiku on county fairs brings a special flavor to the genre, and I can almost smell the smoke from that sulky driver's cigar floating in the damp evening air.

Among the many new poets in this anthology, all with exceptional talents, there are a large number who show not just a promise of greatness to come but have already established a record of accomplishment that makes them substantial figures in the haiku world. Most prominent are Lee Gurga, Dee Evetts, Wally Swist, and Michael Dylan Welch.

Lee Gurga gives us the mystery and wonder of the Midwest: the vast spaces, the rolling prairie, the immense sky, and the majestic rivers. As I recently wrote for the jacket of his latest book, *Fresh Scent*, he "seems destined to forge a fresh poetic heritage for the Midwest." Not only do his haiku let us see the beauty of the land, they allow us to feel the character of its people, which reaches "out of the poems like a warm handshake." In Gurga's sensitive and often humorous poems we discover the heart of America. You'll find a generous selection of them in this anthology.

The following is a part of what I wrote for the back cover of Dee Evetts' *endgrain*: "From the unforgettable comic moment when his waitress flourishes her washrag to that moment of insight into existence as his woodshavings roll along the veranda, the poet presents the reader with a panorama of haiku happenings that both delight and spark awareness." You can sample that panorama here, including the two poems referred to in the quotation.

Wally Swist and Michael Dylan Welch are very dissimilar. Swist is in the tradition of Robert Spiess and John Wills. Though he does not write about Spiess's canoe country or Wills's Tennessee, his haiku are about the same kinds of subject matter. He writes almost solely about the woods and farms of western Massachusetts where he has lived since the early eighties. His style is more like Spiess's, using the juxtaposition of two images to create a single moment. He assisted Spiess as an editor for *Modern Haiku* for a number of years.

Welch intertwines memories of childhood with the present, giving his work an immediacy blended with nostalgia. His images are more urban and domestic than Swist's, and he varies the form more so that his haiku create fresh shapes on the page. Welch is also very important to the haiku community as an editor. His Press Here has published many of the best haiku chapbooks to come out in recent years, and he edited the haiku magazine *Woodnotes* until deciding to discontinue it in order to start a new one, *Tundra*, due this year.

Though not represented by as many haiku as some of those poets I've already mentioned, Vincent Tripi and Carl Patrick write a kind of haiku that seems to involve a whole new way of seeing. Not since Roseliep's has there been a haiku so completely different from what everyone else is writing. Tripi's best work has a mystical quality that reminds me of some passages in Thoreau, whom Tripi regards as a mentor. Many of his haiku moments are unforgettable, like his tracks around the carousel. Carl Patrick can go from the very simplest presentation of the everyday, like his cookie tin, to a wild, seemingly surrealistic view of reality that we see in his hailstone. Washed in the colors of his imagination, things glow in his haiku—but only to disclose their own ineffable essence.

There are so many poets—all the others in this edition—that I would like to praise individually, but you will have the delight of discovering them all as you go through the following pages. However, I would like to take some space here to say a few more words about English-language haiku in general.

The form of haiku that has continued most in favor in English is the otherwise free-form three liner, often written with the second line slightly longer than the first and third. These haiku are usually written in less than seventeen syllables. Though a few poets still write in the 5-7-5 syllable form, this form is now mostly written by schoolchildren as an exercise to learn how to count syllables, by beginners who know little about the true essence of haiku, or by those who just like to have a strict form with which to practice.

The one-line and the two-line haiku, popular in the early and mid-eighties, are now a more occasional phenomenon. The one-line is very hard to write successfully, though some of the most outstanding haiku in English have been in one line. In this anthology, you'll find some of the classic ones, written by poets like John Wills, Marlene Mountain, George Swede, and Matsuo Allard, as well as some great new ones from Alexis Rotella.

There are fewer concrete haiku in this edition than in the last. To work as a haiku a concrete poem has to be simple and direct. It must reveal the essence of whatever image it is trying to evoke immediately, without its graphic configuration calling such attention to itself, or to the writer's ingenuity, as to distract us from that image.

As I learn more and more about haiku, mostly by reading thousands of them, I have come to the conclusion that the greatest haiku are those that take me directly to the haiku moment without calling attention to themselves. When I first read Alan Watts's characterization of haiku as "the wordless poem," I thought it was because a haiku had so few words, but now I believe it goes deeper than that (whether Watts intended it to do so or not). Haiku, for the reader, is wordless because those few words are invisible. We as readers look right through them. There is nothing between us and the moment.

To achieve this goal, certain literary practices common to traditional western poetry are usually avoided by American haiku poets. Such devices as figures of speech or rhyme are rarely employed, for these tend to take away from the thing as it is. The haiku should take us right to the haiku moment and present us with the tree or a leaf, the spring rain or the autumn wind, a rose in a garden or a rusty pick-up under the pines, just as they are—no more, no less. The phrasing and choice of words provide the music of a haiku, which must be as short as a birdsong. Meter is rarely employed. When it is, it is used to create a musical flow that is unobtrusive. For example, if one takes the trouble to listen closely one can detect a subtle current of iambic meter in some of John Wills's haiku. It does not call attention to itself. It is like the faint sound of a breeze helping reveal the haiku moment.

As in previous editions, I have not separated the senryu from the haiku. I like the variety you get by presenting them together, and I think the reader gets more pleasure encountering them unexpectedly—with no warning flags or labels. It is more fun to figure out yourself whether a certain poem is a haiku or senryu. In some the mixture is so even it is hard to decide whether the Nature or human aspect is the more dominant. It could be one or the other.

I hope you'll find that the haiku and senryu in the following pages demonstrate a special magic of language, that they create for you moments of sharp and significant perceptions, coupled with an unspoken awareness of the oneness of the human with nature, and that they spark an intense emotional response. And finally, I hope you'll agree that living in the haiku moment is a poetic experience of the highest order.

Cor van den Heuvel
New York City
Summer 1998

(See Biographical Notes for more books by the poets)

The following books, presses, and organizations are those I consider the most important to English-language haiku. There exist similar sources for all the major languages of the world. Haiku is today an international poetry. To learn about this globe-circling aspect of haiku, the best sources in English are the books listed below by William J. Higginson. His book *Haiku World* is the first international *saijiki* (haiku almanac). It has over a thousand haiku and senryu arranged according to the seasons, with explanations of why certain words and phrases point to particular times of the year. The poems are by more than six hundred poets living in fifty countries and writing in twenty-five languages. All those not written in English appear both in the original language and in English translation. This and a companion volume, *The Haiku Seasons*, which gives a history of the haikai tradition and the Japanese saijiki, are among the most important books published since the last edition of this book.

Others include Hiroaki Sato's superb translations of Matsuo Bashō's *Oku no Hosomichi* and Ozaki Hōsai's haiku and prose. The former is a fully annotated translation of Bashō's major work, and easily the most accessible version in English. The latter makes available the finest work of one of Japan's most important modern haiku poets, Ozaki Hōsai. Hōsai, and another twentieth-century poet, Santōka Taneda (translated by John Stevens), are perhaps closer to us in their free-form style of writing and freedom of spirit than the more famous "pillars" of Japanese haiku.

To better understand the most important pillar of all, Bashō, we now have a book that gives us a wide view of the haikai world that existed during his lifetime. Haruo Shirane's *Traces of Dreams* shows how Bashō and his circle of poets were only a part of a much wider literary phenomenon: they were just one of many competing schools of haikai poetry. Shirane examines the ways in which the master's literary theories changed and developed amidst this mix of tastes and styles and goes on to demonstrate how similar changes are going on in the haiku world today, both in Japan and beyond.

Two of the most important new magazines to appear since the last edition of this book are *Woodnotes* and *South by Southeast*. The first was started in 1989 by the Haiku Poets of Northern California, with Vincent Tripi and Paul O. Williams as the first editors. After a few years, Michael Dylan Welch took over as editor. It became independent of the HPNC in 1996 with Welch still as editor, and he decided in 1997 to let it fold so that he could start a new magazine with a less local focus. The first issue is due sometime in the latter half of 1998. During its existence *Woodnotes* set a new standard for high-quality haiku and related genres like tanka, linked verse, and haibun. The articles were groundbreaking and the quality of the layouts and art work unmatched.

South by Southeast was started about five years ago as an organ of the Southeast Regional Group of the Haiku Society of America, but only came into prominence about a year later under the editorship of Jim Kacian. This too has been an outstanding magazine, being even more comprehensive in its coverage of the world of English-language haiku than *Woodnotes* had been. Kacian is now the new editor of the HSA's *Frogpond*, and Stephen Addis will take over *South by Southeast*. It will continue to be published by Kacian's Red Moon Press, however. The stalwart war-horses of the haiku magazines continue to be the HSA's *Frogpond* and Bob Spiess's *Modern Haiku*. The first has been publishing for twenty years and the second for about thirty.

BOOKS

Amann, Eric W. *The Wordless Poem*. Toronto: Haiku Magazine, 1969.

Ball, Jerry, Garry Gay, and Tom Tico, eds. *The San Francisco Haiku Anthology*. Windsor, CA: Smythe-Waithe Press, 1992.

Beichman, Janine. *Masaoka Shiki*. Boston: Twayne Publishers, 1982.

Brooks, Randy M., and Lee Gurga. *Midwest Haiku Anthology*. Decatur, IL: High/Coo Press (now Brooks Books), 1992.

Blyth, R. H. *Haiku*. Tokyo: Hokuseido Press, 1949–52. 4 vols.

———. *A History of Haiku*. Tokyo: Hokuseido Press, 1963–64. 2 vols.

———. *Japanese Life and Character in Senryu*. Tokyo: Hokuseido Press, 1960.

Cobb, David, and Martin Lucas, eds. *The Iron Book of British Haiku*. North Shields, England: Iron Press, 1998.

Hackett, J. W. *The Zen Haiku and Other Zen Poems of J. W. Hackett*. Tokyo: Japan Publications, 1983 (distributed in the United States by Zen View Distributors, P.O. Box 313, La Honda, CA 94020; in the United Kingdom by The British Haiku Society, see below). On the Web: http://www.fortunecity.com/victorian/literary/205/

Haiku Society of America Twentieth Anniversary Book Committee. *A Haiku Path*. New York: The Haiku Society of America, 1994 (articles from the society's magazine *Frogpond* and a historical look at the development of English-language haiku as reflected in the society's activities during its first twenty years, from 1968 to 1988; full address below).

Henderson, Harold G. *Haiku in English*. New York: Japan Society, 1965 (reprinted by Charles E. Tuttle Company, Rutland, VT, & Tokyo, 1967).

———. *An Introduction to Haiku*. Garden City, NY: Doubleday & Company, 1958.

Higginson, William J. *Haiku World: An International Poetry Almanac*. Tokyo: Kodansha International, 1996.

———. *The Haiku Handbook: How to Write, Share, and Teach Haiku*. New York: McGraw-Hill, 1985 (reprinted by Kodansha International, 1989).

———. *The Haiku Seasons: Poetry of the Natural World*. Tokyo: Kodansha International, 1996.

Howard, Dorothy, and André Duhaime, eds. and trans. *Haïku: Anthologie Canadienne/Canadian Anthology*. Hull, Quebec: Editions Asticou, 1985.

Kacian, Jim, ed. with others. *The Red Moon Anthology* (an annual selection of the best haiku and related works published during the year; so far there have been two, for 1996 and 1997). Winchester, VA: Red Moon Press, 1997, 1998.

Keene, Donald. *World Within Walls: Japanese Literature of the Pre-Modern Era, 1600–1867*. New York: Holt, Rinehart and Winston, 1976.

Miner, Earl. *Japanese Linked Poetry: An Account with Translations of Renga and Haikai Sequences*. Princeton, NJ: Princeton University Press, 1979.

———, and Hiroko Odagiri, trans. *The Monkey's Straw Raincoat and Other Poetry of the Bashō School*. Princeton, NJ: Princeton University Press, 1981.

Ross, Bruce, ed. *Haiku Moment: An Anthology of Contemporary North American Haiku*. Boston, Rutland, VT, & Tokyo: Charles E. Tuttle Company, 1993.

———, ed. *Journey to the Interior: American Versions of Haibun*. Boston: Charles E. Tuttle Company, 1998.

Sato, Hiroaki, trans. *Bashō's Narrow Road* (an annotated translation of Bashō's *Narrow Road to the Interior* and the renga *A Farewell Gift to Sora*, written during the journey, but not included by Bashō in the *Narrow Road*). Berkeley, CA: Stone Bridge Press, 1996.

———. *One Hundred Frogs: From Renga to Haiku to English*. New York: Weatherhill, 1983.

———, trans. *Right under the big sky, I don't wear a hat: The Haiku and Prose of Hōsai Ozaki*. Berkeley, CA: Stone Bridge Press, 1993.

Shirane, Haruo. *Traces of Dreams: Landscape, Cultural Memory, and the Poetry of Bashō*. Stanford, CA: Stanford University Press, 1998.

Stevens, John, trans. *Mountain Tasting: Zen Haiku by Santōka Taneda*. New York: Weatherhill, 1980.

Ueda, Makoto. *Matsuo Bashō*. New York: Twayne, 1970.

———, ed. and trans. *Modern Japanese Haiku: An Anthology*. Toronto: University of Toronto Press, 1976.

Virgilio, Nicholas A. *Selected Haiku*. Sherbrooke, Quebec:

Burnt Lake Press; Windsor, Ontario: Black Moss Press, 1988 (available in the United States from The Nick Virgilio Haiku Association, see below).

Wills, John. *Reed Shadows* (Haiku). Co-published by Black Moss Press, Windsor, Ontario, and Burnt Lake Press, Sherbrooke, Quebec, 1987.

Yasuda, Kenneth. *The Japanese Haiku*. Rutland, VT, & Tokyo: Charles E. Tuttle Company, 1957.

MAGAZINES AND HAIKU PRESSES

AHA Books, Jane Reichhold, editor and publisher, P.O. Box 1250, Gualala, CA 95445.

Brooks Books (High/Coo Press), Randy M. Brooks, editor and publisher, 4634 Hale Drive, Decatur, IL 62526.

Burnt Lake Press, Rod Willmot, editor and publisher, 535 Irène-Couture, Sherbrooke, Quebec, J1L 1Y8.

Frogpond (magazine of the Haiku Society of America), Jim Kacian, editor, P.O. Box 2461, Winchester, VA 22604-1661.

From Here Press, William J. Higginson, editor and publisher, P.O. Box 2740, Santa Fe, NM 87504-2740.

High/Coo Press (see Brooks Books).

Iron Press, 5 Marden Terrace, Cullercoats, North Shields, Northumberland, NE30 4Pd, England, UK.

King's Road Press, Marco Fraticelli, editor and publisher, 148 King's Road, Pointe Claire, Quebec, H9R 4H4.

Modern Haiku, Robert Spiess, editor and publisher, P.O. Box 1752, Madison, WI 53701-1752.

Press Here, Michael Dylan Welch, editor and publisher, 248

Beach Park Blvd., Foster City, CA 94404.

proof press, Dorothy Howard, editor and publisher, 67 Court, Aylmer, Quebec J9H 4M1, Canada.

RAW NerVZ (see proof press).

Red Moon Press, Jim Kacian, editor and publisher, P.O. Box 2461, Winchester, VA 22604-1661.

Smythe-Waithe Press, 9632 Berkshire Way, Windsor, CA 95492.

Tiny Poems Press, John Sheirer, editor and publisher, Asnuntuck Community-Technical College, 170 Elm Street, Enfield, CT 06082.

Tundra (see Press Here).

ORGANIZATIONS

The British Haiku Society, Sinodun, Shalford, Braintree, Essex, CM7 5HN, England, UK.

Haiku Canada, 67 Court, Aylmer, Quebec J9H 4M1.

The Haiku Society of America, c/o Japan Society, 333 East 47th Street, New York, NY 10017.

The Nick Virgilio Haiku Association, 1092 Niagara Road, Camden, NJ 08104.

Note: When writing to magazines, presses, or organizations enclose a stamped self-addressed envelope; if writing one in another country, enclose an international reply coupon, available at the post office.

PREFACE TO
THE SECOND EDITION

Someone, probably thinking of Bashō's famous haiku about the-sound-of-a-frog-jumping-into-an-old-pond, once likened the English-language haiku movement to a small puddle far from the mainstream of poetry. If so, the puddle is doing very well on its own. While the mainstream moves, for the most part, sluggishly through gray fogs of obscurity and intellectualization, the puddle is ablaze with color and light—as a glance through this book will show.

There are no signs of its ever drying up—on the contrary, it seems to be springfed—and the "frogs" who inhabit it are singing songs filled with original imagery, stark beauty, sparkling wit, intense emotion, peaceful calm, and acute awareness.

This edition of *The Haiku Anthology* contains around seven hundred haiku, senryu, and related works—about five hundred more than there were in the First Edition, which was published in the spring of 1974. Extraordinary things have happened to haiku since then—due, primarily, to the innovative, fresh approaches brought to the genre by the poets represented in this book. Haiku will become what the poets make it, to paraphrase the late Harold G. Henderson,[1] and our haiku literature is as rich and varied as it is because such poets as Anita Virgil, Alan Pizzarelli, Michael McClintock, Marlene Mountain, George Swede, Raymond Roseliep, John Wills, Gary Hotham, Alexis Rotella, and others have led the way into directions of accomplishment undreamed of in the early years of the movement.

These accomplishments are also, indirectly, the result of work of scholars and translators of Japanese literature, such as Henderson himself. In recent years new books by Makoto Ueda, Earl Miner, Hiroaki Sato, Burton Watson, and Donald Keene have deepened our understanding of Japanese haiku and its related genres, significantly affecting how we write their counterparts in English.

In the years between editions there have been three major developments: the emergence of the one-liner as

[1] One of the pioneer scholar/translators of haiku, Harold Henderson died in 1974, shortly after the First Edition of the *Anthology* was published.

a common form for haiku and senryu; the growing practice of writing longer works, such as sequences and renga; and the increasing importance of human relationships, especially sex and love, as subject matter.

Though many poets had been moving toward more freedom for the haiku form in the early seventies, especially away from the restrictions of the 5-7-5 syllable count, it was only in the latter half of the decade that the one-line form became more than an occasional exception to the three-line "rule." The three-line form, with no set syllable count, remains the standard, but some of the best haiku in English have been written in one line, and the form is now widely used.[2]

Three people were initially responsible for gaining its general acceptance: Marlene Mountain (formerly known as Marlene Wills) was the first to write good one-line haiku with some regularity; Hiroaki Sato translated Japanese haiku into one-liners and lent "legitimacy" to the writing of original one-liners in English;[3] and Matsuo Allard furthered the cause of the

[2] The First Edition had only a single one-liner, Michael Segers' "in the eggshell after the chick has hatched."

[3] Sato's one-line haiku translations started appearing in magazines in 1976, and over six hundred are in the anthology *From the Country of Eight Islands* (1981). Sato also lent confirmation to an earlier conclusion by William J. Higginson, which appeared in a small book called *Itadakimasu* in 1971, that ten to fourteen syllables in English, rather than seventeen, most closely match the sound length of the seventeen *onji* in a traditional Japanese haiku.

one-liner by writing polemical essays in its favor, editing and publishing several short-lived but important magazines devoted to it, publishing chapbooks of them, and by writing them himself.[4]

The most common argument for one-liners is that the Japanese write haiku in one vertical line or column and therefore we should write in one line also, but of course horizontally in the Western style. Strict "three-liner" advocates argue that since the Japanese haiku breaks into three parts because of the 5-7-5 syllable (*onji*) form—a pattern that occurs naturally in the Japanese language—the only way to parallel it in English is to write in three lines. Of course many poets write in one form or the other simply because they think the particular poem they are writing works better in that form.

There has also been some experimentation with two-line haiku—Bob Boldman has probably had the most success with them—but they are still quite rare. A few poets have tried writing English-language tanka. These five-line poems have usually been most successful when done in the introspective style of Takuboku Ishikawa (1885–1912) rather than in the traditional lyric manner.

[4] Matsuo Allard's press was first called Sun-Lotus and later became The First Haiku Press. As far as can be determined, the press is no longer in existence. Matsuo Allard also used the name R. Clarence Matsuo-Allard.

Longer forms in the shape of sequences have been a part of the haiku scene since at least the sixties, and a few short ones were included in the First Edition, but they have increased in popularity in recent years. While most sequences have been made up of haiku or senryu which can stand alone as poems themselves—at least their authors intended them to have that ability—Marlene Mountain and Alexis Rotella have written a kind in which the individual elements, though firmly rooted in haiku and senryu, depend largely on their context for their effectiveness, and only one or two out of several may be able to stand alone. Similar sequences of haiku or tanka that depend on context for meaning have been written in Japanese. They are called *rensaku*.

An attempt at English-language renga was published as early as 1968 in *Haiku Magazine*, but it wasn't till the mid-seventies that the form became of any importance. Also called "linked-verse poem" or "renku," renga were originally written at a live session, like a jazz improvisation, but in English have most often been done through the mails, with two, three, or more poets writing links in turn.

William J. Higginson and Tadashi Kondo played seminal roles in awakening interest in renga early in 1976 with discussions at the Haiku Society of America. These were recorded in the society's newsletter, and later that year *Haiku Magazine* put out an issue devoted to renga and haibun (prose pieces written in the spirit of haiku). In the late seventies and early eighties, Marlene Mountain and Hiroaki Sato participated in a number of renga that appeared in *Cicada* and in the Haiku Society's *Frogpond*. Sato has been one of the most influential figures in American haiku in recent years (he was president of the Haiku Society of America for three terms, 1979–81). His book *One Hundred Frogs: From Renga to Haiku to English* (1983) gives an informative and entertaining history of Japanese renga, along with a brief account of English-language renga and a small anthology of the latter. In Japan haiku originated when the hokku of *haikai no renga* began to be written as an independent poem. The process has been reversed in the West. Renga developed here when haiku poets started looking for ways to extend the haiku into longer forms. Its importance for this anthology is that the practice of writing renga has helped stimulate innovation in the writing of haiku and senryu and has encouraged the exchange of ideas and a sense of community among poets by bringing them in closer contact with one another.

Another longer form is the haibun. These prose pieces—which usually contain one or more haiku—have been tried occasionally in English, but except for some parts of two novels by Jack Kerouac little of significance has appeared yet. In several passages in *Desolation Angels* and *The Dharma Bums*, Kerouac has come closer than any other writer in English to the terse, elliptical, nature-inspired prose that characterizes the genre. His descriptions of his experiences alone on Desolation Mountain have the whirling brevity and vivid immediacy of some of Bashō's great haibun. Unfortunately, the few haiku he includes are not of comparable merit.

The last major development involves subject matter. Though there were in the First Edition a few haiku or senryu dealing with sex—some of Michael McClintock's come immediately to mind—they were rare exceptions. Sex, love, and the whole range of human emotions and relationships have now become fairly common themes. Rod Willmot, one of the movement's most important critics and one of Canada's leading haiku poets, calls most of these poems "psychological haiku"; those specifically about sex he has called "erotic haiku." "Serious senryu" would be more accurate, I think, for most of them. Instead of recreating a moment of awareness in which human nature is related to nature, they give one a moment of awareness about one's own inner feelings or one's relationships with other human beings.

Senryu began as comic verse, but that does not mean it has to be called haiku when it becomes serious. It seems useful to me to keep the two genres distinct in somewhat the same way the Japanese do—haiku relates to Nature and the seasons, senryu relates to human nature. Traditionally, the Japanese have ensured this by insisting that to be a haiku the poem must have a season word (*kigo*), while a senryu does not. They have always had the same form. It is the subject matter that determines the genre—not the form, and not whether the subject matter is looked at humorously or not. Haiku itself began as a kind of humorous verse, and one can still write a funny haiku.

In recent years, more and more writers have been creating comic and serious senryu that rival the best haiku in the depth of insight they reveal and the emotional richness they convey. Michael McClintock, who edited a magazine (*seer ox*) in the mid-seventies devoted to senryu, and Alan Pizzarelli, who wrote many comic senryu about the same time, were probably the first to spark significant interest in the genre—though Clement Hoyt and a few others had written fine senryu earlier. Recently George Swede, a Canadian, has become one of the best senryu writers in English—of both the humorous and the serious kinds. He is a highly original writer of haiku as well, and his work in both genres has influenced a number of other poets. In the United States, Marlene Mountain (particularly in her sequences), Alexis Rotella, and Bob Boldman—among others—have led the way in bringing psychology, or more subjectivity, into both haiku and senryu. Rotella has polished this facet of the art with such brilliance that she has become in only a few years one of the stars in the growing constellation of out-standing haiku/senryu poets.

As in the First Edition, I have not tried to separate the senryu from the haiku in this book—not because of the slight difficulty in deciding which is which, for a few do overlap, but because an interesting variety, contrast, and resonance can result from their juxtaposition.

Though one-liners, longer works, and serious senryu are the most obvious, widespread developments, there have been many other successful explorations of the possibilities of haiku and its related genres. Usually these have been accomplished by the individual genius, or style, of a particular poet, from the minimalist and "unaloud" pieces of Marlene Mountain to the extended haiku and "sound" poems of Pizzarelli. Mountain had published little in the haiku magazines before exploding on the scene in 1976 with her book, *the old tin roof*. Since then she has figured prominently in the movement, and her inventive and powerful writing has helped to shape many of the changes that have taken place. Though Pizzarelli had a few poems in the First Edition of the anthology, he has since become the clown/magician of the haiku world, materializing an amazing array of word-wonders that brings the wise craziness of the poet/monks of the past into the modern world of chrome and neon.

Raymond Roseliep, another sui-generis poet, had

tried his hand at haiku in the early seventies, but his main work and reputation then was in traditionally Western genres. When he later devoted his craft to haiku, he kept a Western flavor in it which makes it hard to say exactly what his marvelously witty and off-the-wall creations are—William J. Higginson has resorted to the word "liepku." One of the most prolific poets in the movement, Roseliep left us a large body of these sparkling and delightful poems which undeniably belong to haiku/senryu before he died in 1983.

In fact, all the voices in this book have unique qualities: Gary Hotham is a master of what might be called the "plain," or "subtle," haiku, so ordinary that unless you are especially alert you may miss the resonance stirring beneath the simple image of, say, an overdue book or a paper cup; Martin Shea has a dramatist's skill in setting a scene that tells a story—his images lead us into a narrative that continues on in our minds after the poem is read; Penny Harter zooms in for close-ups of a cat's whisker or the toe of a boot with such startling clarity and effective cropping they loom into a sudden indefinable significance; Scott Montgomery's work often has a surreal, dreamlike aura about it; Arizona Zipper has a wry, earthy, down-home humor; and so on.

Canadian poets have long played an important role in the English-language haiku movement, especially

Eric Amann, who edited *Haiku* and *Cicada*, perhaps English-language haiku's most influential magazines.[5] They are still unsurpassed for excellence in both content and design, though both have ceased publication—the last, *Cicada*, in 1981. Amann and Rod Willmot, both of whom were in the First Edition, and George Swede are Canada's leading haiku poets. Among the other new voices from the Canadian part of the "puddle," LeRoy Gorman's and Chuck Brickley's are perhaps the brightest.

All the major American figures in the First Edition appear again in this one—including Foster Jewell, J. W. Hackett, Nicholas Virgilio, Robert Spiess, John Wills, Michael McClintock, William J. Higginson, Anita Virgil, and O. Mabson Southard (then writing under the name Mabelsson Norway). Several of these poets have been very active in the haiku movement in the years between editions. Michael McClintock was especially busy in the mid-seventies with his Seer Ox Press—putting out the magazine and several chapbooks by various poets, while also writing and publishing work of his own. Robert Spiess took over the editorship of *Modern Haiku* magazine in 1978 (from

[5] Two important anthologies of Canadian haiku have appeared: George Swede's *Canadian Haiku Anthology* (1979) and *Haiku: Anthologie Canadienne/Canadian Anthology* (1985), edited by Dorothy Howard and André Duhaime, a bilingual collection of French-language and English-language haiku.

Kay Mormino, who started it in 1969), keeping it the stable, smooth-sailing, general arbiter of the haiku scene it had always been—where the conservatives and radicals of the movement can both be heard but moderation predominates. His poetry has taken on a darker tone in recent years, yet it still glows with keenly perceived moments from the world of forest and stream.

William J. Higginson was a sort of guru to the haiku movement in the early and mid-seventies. He left the puddle for a time, but became active there again in the eighties. He and Willmot are probably our most astute critics. As well as being a critic/poet Higginson is a scholar/translator of Japanese literature. In his recent *The Haiku Handbook: How to Write, Share, and Teach Haiku* (1985), he gives one of the clearest delineations of what a haiku does and how it does it that exists in English. He also presents a comprehensive picture of the development of both Japanese and world haiku from its beginnings to the present, succinctly condensing and incorporating with his own translations, research, and analyses the most important new information about haiku and its related genres from the large body of scholarly works on Japanese literature of the past twenty-five years. It is an indispensable companion volume to the great works of Blyth and Henderson.

Nicholas Virgilio's work continues to illuminate the

shadows of death. Adding to the elegiac series of haiku about his brother, who died in Vietnam, he has created a moving testament to the power of art and love to rescue the memory of a loved one from the blankness of death. The autumn wind, which somehow evokes trust and fear at the same time, blows through his haiku with a strange consolatory power that is unforgettable.

"A reclusive and fiercely independent spirit," J. W. Hackett has not been directly involved with the haiku movement since the sixties, when his work appeared in the haiku magazines, but his haiku continue to attract new readers and writers to the genre. They are probably better known than those of any other non-Japanese poet and have been praised by R. H. Blyth, Alan Watts, and Jack Kerouac. However, for more than a decade now he has been mainly interested in writing longer poems, a number of which are in *The Zen Haiku and Other Zen Poems of J. W. Hackett* (1983), a book that, happily, also contains all the haiku from his long-popular *The Way of Haiku*.

Between 1974 and 1980, Foster Jewell produced nine more of his enchanting chapbooks of haiku, two of them in collaboration with his wife, Rhoda de Long Jewell. While evoking vivid images of the woodlands, mountains, and deserts he loved, Jewell also had a way of summoning the spirit of nature into his haiku so that you felt its presence—in the sound of thunder along a beach or in the silence of a moonrise. In 1984 he passed away into the silences he wrote so intimately about.

O. Mabson Southard remains a mysterious figure, like his changing name, and much to the regret of the many admirers of his haiku there has been no new work by him in the haiku magazines for several years now. He has, it is said, recently turned his mind to other concerns, including the study of mathematics. The sharp clarity and depth of his images—the rocks and tree coming out of the mist in his well-known "old rooster" haiku, the loon's cry crossing the still lake, the sparrow knocking snow from a fence-rail, the dogwood petal carrying its moonlight into the darkness—these and many more will ensure that his name (or names) will endure as long as there are readers of haiku.

Anita Virgil's stature, like Southard's, becomes more ensured as we see how her haiku continue to shine as brightly as ever though the years go by: the flickering light on the pine bark, that feeling of sinking through the snow-crust, the spring peepers, the shadows on the dinner plates. Virgil, too, was silent for a few years but in the early eighties started writing again. One of the first of these new haiku was "holding you." It won first prize in a special erotic-haiku contest conducted by *Cicada* that resulted in the book *Erotic Haiku* (1983), edited by Rod Willmot.

John Wills has been one of the most productive

poets in the movement—especially in the years since the last edition—and he has found a way of haiku that is closer to nature, more resonant with its mystery and wonder, than the work of perhaps anyone else writing today in whatever genre. With only a few syllables, he creates haiku of such clarity and purity they seem to have come from the hand of nature itself.

There are some poets in this book that should have been in the earlier edition but were not. Jack Kerouac, for example. He was one of the first to write haiku in English, and to do so in a distinctively modern, American style, using a colloquial idiom and everyday, local images rather than turning out imitation Japanese poems about cherry blossoms.

The medium for the writers of haiku in English has continued to be the haiku magazines and the small presses that publish haiku chapbooks. They are the movement. *Leanfrog*, a haiku newsletter published on the West Coast, listed nineteen magazines in 1982 that were accepting haiku, with many of them specializing exclusively in haiku literature. In addition, it listed seven haiku societies. The haiku magazines come and go like most small-press ventures, but a few have managed to publish for several years. The most important magazines and presses still publishing are included in the Book List.

After about twenty-five years of English-language haiku, do we know what a haiku is? There seems to be no general consensus—which may be a sign of its health and vitality. There is still much talk about awareness and perception—less about Zen and the Infinite. Hiroaki Sato, especially, has tried to get the Zen out of haiku, saying that Western critics have been responsible for the association and that Japanese haiku poets have much simpler intentions than to try to give their readers "enlightenment." "Haiku have been written," he writes, "to congratulate, to praise, to describe, to express gratitude, wit, cleverness, disappointment, resentment, or what have you, but rarely to convey enlightenment" *(One Hundred Frogs*, p. 131).

It is said that Bashō toward the end of his life felt his love for haiku might be a worldly attachment standing in the way of self-realization—but, try as he would, he could not give it up. What did haiku give him that made it so hard to abandon—even for the promise of spiritual peace? It must have been more than just the opportunity to express gratitude or resentment, or the chance to congratulate or describe. His disciple Dohō's explanation of what the Master meant by his famous saying "Learn about a pine tree from a pine tree, and about a bamboo plant from a bamboo plant" suggests an answer:

> What he meant was that a poet should detach the mind from his own personal self. Nevertheless some poets interpret the word "learn" in their own

ways and never really "learn." For "learn" means to enter into the object, perceive its delicate life and feel its feelings, whereupon a poem forms itself. A lucid description of the object is not enough; unless the poem contains feelings which have spontaneously emerged from the object, it will show the object and the poet's self as two separate entities, making it impossible to attain a true poetic sentiment. The poem will be artificial, for it is composed by the poet's personal self.[6]

Now Dohō is not explaining enlightenment, but neither is he explaining how to "praise" or "describe"—in fact, he states that description is not enough. The process he does set forth, however, sounds very similar to the way Zen Buddhists describe the path to enlightenment: achieving detachment from the self, becoming one with existence. If you become one with something other than yourself, leaving self behind, isn't that a way to know, or to at least catch a glimpse of, the truth that all existence is one? If that's not enlightenment, it certainly seems like a step in the right direction. Of course, true enlightenment is said to require giving up *all* attachments—so the monk must also give up those things that have helped him along the way, including his koans, his sitting, and

[6] From Makoto Ueda's *Matsuo Bashō*, pp. 167–168.

even his desire for enlightenment itself. So because a Buddhist poet feels he must give up poetry doesn't necessarily mean that the poetry wasn't useful along the way. R. H. Blyth has written:

> A haiku is the expression of a temporary enlightenment, in which we see into the life of things. . . . It is a way in which the cold winter rain, the swallows of evening, even the very day in its hotness, and the length of the night become truly alive, share in our humanity, speak their own silent and expressive language.[7]

Since writing the passage quoted earlier, Sato seems to have taken a new look at this question. In a talk called "Bashō and the Concept of 'The Way' in Japanese Poetry," given to the Haiku Society of America in December 1983, he quoted Bashō as saying that "poetry writing is another vehicle for entering the True Way (*makoto no michi*)" and pointed out that the "True Way" means Buddhism. Bashō, who "trained in Zen," apparently felt, at least part of the time, that he was on a spiritual path when he wrote haiku.[8]

Ultimately haiku eludes definition. It is "always evolving, burgeoning, growing," Rod Willmot writes in a recent letter—and it may be a good thing, he adds,

[7] *Haiku*, Vol. I, pp. 270, 272.
[8] *Frogpond*, VI, 4 (1983).

if, rather than working toward a restrictive definition, we continue in our present direction, where haiku poets are creating "a whole variety of poetics and criticisms, coexisting rather than competing."

That variety can be experienced in the following pages.

Cor van den Heuvel
New York City
Spring 1986

INTRODUCTION TO
THE FIRST EDITION

Until now, the poets represented in this anthology have been largely "invisible." Though some of them have been writing haiku for nearly two decades or longer, their work has flowered practically unnoticed—their only recognition coming from the small world of the haiku magazines. The movement of which they are a part, however, has now reached a point where its accomplishments can no longer be ignored.

Haiku in English got its real start in the fifties, when an avid interest in Japanese culture and religion swept the postwar United States.[1] Growing out of the increased

[1] The Imagists, and those who followed them, had no real understanding of haiku. Because they had no adequate transla-

contacts with Japan through the Occupation and a spiritual thirst for religious and artistic fulfillment, this interest centered on art, literature, and Zen Buddhism. Alan Watts, Donald Keene, D. T. Suzuki, the Beats, and others all contributed to both arousing and feeding this interest, but it was R. H. Blyth's extraordinary four-volume work *Haiku* (published between 1949 and 1952), Kenneth Yasuda's *The Japanese Haiku* (1957), and Harold G. Henderson's *An Introduction to Haiku* (1958) that provided for the first time the solid foundation necessary for the creation of haiku in English.[2]

In the late fifties and early sixties, the seed began to germinate, and a few poets across the country began to write haiku with an awareness and understanding of its possibilities.

Within five years after the publication of Hender-

---

tions or critical analyses available, they failed to see the spiritual depth haiku embodies, or the unity of man and nature it reveals. English-language haiku owes practically nothing to their experiments except in the sense that all modern poetry owes them a debt for their call for concision and clarity in language.

[2] Henderson published a small book on Japanese haiku, *The Bamboo Broom*, in 1934, in which he recognized the possibility of English haiku. But the time was not ripe. (There were exceptions: Clement Hoyt began studying Zen in 1936 with Nyogen Senzaki, the man who "taught me the haiku," and Yasuda was writing haiku in English in the thirties, publishing some as "Experiments in English" in *A Pepper Pod*, 1947.)

son's book, a magazine was started by James Bull in Platteville, Wisconsin, devoted solely to English-language haiku: *American Haiku* (1963). The first issue was dedicated to Henderson and included a letter from him to the editors, which said in part: "If there is to be a real 'American Haiku' we must—by trial and error—work out our own standards. . . . One of the great functions *American Haiku* could perform is that of being a forum for the expression of divergent opinions." J. W. Hackett, Nicholas Virgilio, Mabelsson Norway (O Southard), and Larry Gates were among the contributors to that first issue.[3] The magazine was published twelve times in the next five years, ceasing publication in May 1968. Later that year, under the auspices of the Japan Society, the Haiku Society of America was founded to promote the writing and appreciation of haiku.

In the meantime, three new haiku magazines had emerged, all of which are still publishing. Jean Calkins started *Haiku Highlights and Other Small Poems* (now called *Dragonfly: A Quarterly of Haiku Highlights*) in Kanona, New York, in 1965. Though the work it published was undistinguished for a long time, in recent years it has printed significant articles on

---

[3] Among those appearing in the second issue were Robert Spiess, Virginia Brady Young, Clement Hoyt, and Elizabeth Searle Lamb.

haiku by William J. Higginson, Michael McClintock, and others. In 1967 two haiku magazines appeared that were to carry on the work begun by *American Haiku*: *Haiku West*, edited by Leroy Kanterman in New York City, and *Haiku*, edited by Eric Amann in Toronto, Canada. (*Haiku* is now edited by William J. Higginson in Paterson, New Jersey.) Both have printed high-quality haiku, and *Haiku* has especially demonstrated a willingness to experiment with haiku form and presentation.

There are now at least five English-language haiku magazines being published in the United States, with others in England and Australia. In fact, haiku are being written all over the world—in German, French, Spanish, Portuguese, Italian, and other languages, as well as English and, of course, Japanese.[4]

In the midst of this proliferating interest and activity with haiku throughout the world, the "literary world"—critics and poets alike—continues to see English-language haiku either as worthless fragments, blank and incomprehensible, or as little more than examples of a form of light verse whose only use is as an educational aid to interest children in poetry.[5] Such

[4] See Gary Brower's annotated bibliography, *Haiku in Western Languages* (1972).

[5] There are exceptions. A few well-known poets have tried to write haiku, but none has seen it as a principal "way" or direction for their work. Gary Snyder, though he was one of the first to try

attitudes may have been excused in the early years—thousands of bad poems were published under the name of haiku—but in the last few years the proportion of good haiku to bad has been at least the same as in any other kind of poetry.

One can only conclude that such critics have not looked deeply enough into the literature available on the Japanese haiku and its esthetic traditions—or simply do not know haiku in English. Haiku is a poetry of simplicity and suggestion new to Western literature. It has been called the "wordless poem,"[6] and is often so bare as to seem meaningless to the uninitiated. Yet its few words have such an ontological immediacy that the sensitive reader can almost reach out and touch the things they describe. However commonplace the image, it is *now* in one of those timeless moments when it flashes forth an unspoken message of the one-

---

writing haiku in English with an understanding of Japanese haiku (as early as 1952), has never concentrated his poetic energies in that direction. Jack Kerouac, the Beat novelist, was also an early practitioner of haiku and probably came closer than any of the Beat poets to its essence. But it remained a footnote to his other work. More recently, Hayden Carruth, Robert Kelly, John Hollander, and some other recognized poets have experimented with short poems which derive from the form of haiku, but show little or no conception of the haiku's true nature.

[6] By Alan Watts. Eric Amann wrote an exceptionally fine book on haiku using this phrase for the title. It appeared as a special issue of *Haiku* in 1969.

ness of existence. It does so in the silence that surrounds the words. Blyth has called haiku "an open door which looks shut," because it takes an intuitive awareness to see that moment of perception which lies just over the threshold. The reader must be an equal partner in the creative process—the slightest shift of focus or mood can close the door again. Aware readers are increasing, however, and the "visibility" of haiku in English will depend on their perception.

Haiku in English is still in the process of finding its "way." Beyond a general agreement that haiku should be short, concise, and immediate (or brief, simple, and direct, etc.), individual poets may often diverge widely in their conceptions of what a haiku is and how one is created. One of the most fundamental questions raised about haiku has been: is it basically a religious or an esthetic experience?

A number of those who favor the religious, or as some prefer to say, spiritual side of this question relate haiku to the philosophy of Zen. J. W. Hackett and Eric Amann have been spokesmen for this view, which follows the "teachings" of R. H. Blyth. Citing Bashō— "Haiku is simply what is happening in this place, at this moment"—Hackett emphasizes haiku as a "way" of life, rather than as literature. In his book *The Way of Haiku* (1969),[7] the poet states:

[7] One of the very few haiku poets with a book readily obtainable at bookstores, Hackett alone has had a large body of

I have written in the conviction that the best haiku are created from direct and immediate experience with nature, and that this intuitive experience can be expressed in any language. In essence I regard haiku as fundamentally existential and experiential, rather than literary. There are, of course, important structural and artistic considerations involved in the expression of the haiku experience . . .

In *Haiku in English* (1965), Henderson contrasts Hackett's approach ("what may loosely be called the Bashō school") with that of Nicholas Virgilio and others who stress imaginative creation—that is, the artistic role of the poet as a maker of imagined scenes as well as experienced ones, exemplified in Japanese haiku by Buson. Some of the poets who lean toward this view may believe their work is ultimately based on actual experience too, in the sense that even their imagined scenes are put together from things they have known. And since it is possible for *readers* to experience a "haiku moment" through words, even though they may never have encountered it in reality,

---

work available for several years. A number of the poets in this anthology have, however, been published by small presses (see Biographical Notes). [In 1983 Hackett published *The Zen Haiku and Other Zen Poems of J. W. Hackett*, which is a revised and enlarged edition of *The Way of Haiku*. It too contains the passage quoted above.]

there are *poets* who claim they can discover such moments in words during the creative process.

There is also the question of "natural speech" (artless) as opposed to language which uses poetic techniques. An argument against a too "literary" approach is R. H. Blyth's admonition that a bejewelled finger distracts from what it is pointing at. But it is well to keep in mind that a deformed finger can be distracting too, and may even point the wrong way.

The distinction between haiku and senryu, which are structurally similar, has also been a subject of controversy. Haiku is said to relate human nature to nature in general, while senryu is concerned primarily with human nature and is often humorous; but it is hard to draw the line.[8]

There are other differences among the haiku poets: there are the 5-7-5ers who believe haiku should be written in three lines of 5-7-5 syllables; then there are those who think the norm for English should be less than seventeen syllables to more closely approximate the actual length of seventeen Japanese *onji* (sound-symbols), which are generally shorter than English syllables. Still others, like Michael McClintock, are for a "liberated haiku"—rejecting syllable-counting com-

---

[8] I have not tried to separate the senryu from the haiku in this book.

pletely. There is the problem of subjectivity in haiku: is it allowable at all, and if so to what degree? And, on the other hand, is complete objectivity really possible?—and so on.

These "disputes" among the poets don't prevent them from appreciating each other's work and are actually a way of answering Henderson's call to "work out our own standards." "Haiku" may be on its way to becoming a much broader term than it has been in the past. This may or may not be a good thing; but while some are working to broaden the concept, there are others who are moving toward a simpler, purer, deeper kind of haiku—and even a few who are finding ways to create poems which do both at once. Japanese haiku has survived countless controversies in its centuries-old history, and haiku in English will too. As Henderson says, what haiku in English will become "will depend primarily on the poets who write them."[9]

A great diversity lies in the pages ahead. But though these poets are all moving along individual paths, they are all following the haiku "way." The variety of their voices should delight us as much as the oneness they reveal enlightens us. For the joy of life is to be able to see it anew each moment. These haiku moments await only your contribution of awareness.

[9] *Haiku in English.*

Here you'll find the strange landscapes of Nicholas Virgilio, which, while remaining part of the real world, take us on a surrealistic trip to the source of the life force in a lily or to the mystery of death in the headlights of a funeral procession; or the simple wonders of J. W. Hackett, where a caterpillar or a small cloud of gnats can take us to the core of existence simply by being what they are *now;* the daring experimentation of William J. Higginson or Anita Virgil, who both find new visceral possibilities in words; the muse-guided nature sensitivity of Mabelsson Norway, whose word-spells can call trees and rocks out of a timeless mist; the pure simplicity of Robert Spiess, the subtle clarity of whose images resonates again and again through the natural juxtaposition of the barest aspects of nature; the rich, fertile earth and living waters of John Wills; the haunting silences of Foster Jewell; the fresh virtuosity, sensual vigor, and delicacy of perception of Michael McClintock; and many more, all with their own individual voices, their own way of looking at the world through haiku.

There are undoubtedly poets and haiku missing from the following pages that belong here, but here at least is a representative selection—here is haiku in English becoming visible.

New York City
June 1973

THE HAIKU ANTHOLOGY

ERIC AMANN

Billboards
wet
in spring
rain . . .

The circus tent
  all folded up:
    October mist . . .

Snow falling
  on the empty parking-lot:
    Christmas Eve . . .

A night train passes:
pictures of the dead are trembling
on the mantelpiece

The names of the dead
sinking deeper and deeper
into the red leaves

Winter burial:
a stone angel points his hand
at the empty sky

Sunset:
one last parachute
floats slowly down

spring is here
    the cat's muddy paw prints
    on the windowsill

sun behind the hills
    the fisherman ships his oars
        and drifts into shore

longing to be near her
i remember my shirt
hanging in her closet

the telephone
rings only once
    autumn rain

freshly fallen snow
opening a new package
of typing paper

the evening star
just above the snow the tip
of an alder bush

northern lights shimmer
a saw-whet piping
on the distant shore

moss-hung trees
a deer moves into
the hunter's silence

snowflakes fill
the eye of the eagle
fallen totem pole

snow silenced town
then the stillness broken
whistle of the train

skinny young men
grouped around the car's raised hood
spring's here

a dozen red roses
the box lightly stained
by spring rain

through binoculars
    a woman looking at me
through binoculars

next to the wanted poster
the man with the goatee

tugging and begging
at the end of his leash
the dog's owner

mirror   my face where I left it

leaves blowing into a sentence

mist,
panties on the line

in the doll's
head
news clippings

in the heat
admiring the shade in the blouse

face wrapping a champagne glass

a moment in the box of jade

in the temple
a
heartbeat

touching the ashes of my father

day darkens   in the shell

a fin
grazing on restless stars

the priest
          his shadow caught
   on a nail.

JANUARY FIRST
the fingers of the prostitute cold

i end in shadow

long meeting
I study the pattern
embossed on the napkin

morning surf
a dog fills the sky
with seagulls

sheet lightning:
the face near the top
of the ferris wheel

the puppet
leaning from his booth
blinks at the rain

outside the pub
the sailor
faces the wind

deserted wharf
the mime bows
to the moon

After washing up
putting a warm plate back
in the cold cupboard

someone's newspaper
drifts with the snow
at 4 a.m.

waiting:
dry snowflakes fall
against the headlights

an empty elevator
opens
closes

end of the hour—
    twilight shadows obscure
    the therapist's face

finding their line
    in the deepening fog
    a dozen pelicans

sudden shower
in the empty park
a swing still swinging

saying good-bye
snow melting
from the roof tiles

Through the slats
of the outhouse door
Everest!

Farm country back road:
just like them i lift one finger
from the steering wheel

Waiting to see
the odometer's big change . . .
                missed it!

        going the same way . . .
exchanging looks with the driver
of the hearse

daybreak—
from the bread truck's roof
frost swirls

the plumber
kneeling in our tub
—talking to himself

sidewalk sale—
wind twists a lifetime
guarantee tag

light snow . . .
the students study
in silence

red geraniums
     rips in the awning
    leak sunlight

kaleidoscope
the little sound of a star
shattering

On the mountain slope
the stillness of white pines
in the falling snow

A crow caws:
in the silence of the woods
the flap of its wings

beyond
stars beyond
star

in the dark lobby
of the residential hotel
a feeling of autumn

on my return
she brings blue plums
on a white plate

the silent crowd
waiting for the fountain
to rise again

it is growing dark,
no one has come to the door,
and still the dog barks

subway woman asleep
picked daisies
in her hand

between the twirlers
and the marching band
the missing child

MIKE DILLON

Spring afternoon:
the barber spins me around
towards the mirror

The last kid picked
running his fastest
to right field

August night:
the lamplit quiet
as our children draw

autumn night:
following the flashlight beam
through the rain

Deep snow:
peeling potatoes—
dark earth on my hands

Snow at dusk:
our pot of tea
steeps   slowly   darker

a drift of snow
in the picnic table's shadow
first day of spring

the white of her neck
as she lifts her hair for me
to undo her dress

the thousand colors
in her plain brown hair—
morning sunshine

frog pond—
a leaf falls in
without a sound

Thick window frost—
through a melted finger hole
blue sky

Shielding his eyes
with his baseball glove . . .
first geese

A steady wind blows
cloud shadows up the mountain
and off the cliff

Between two mountains
the wings of a gliding hawk
balancing sunlight

long July afternoon
at the railroad crossing
the train goes on and on

back from vacation
I let traces of sand
remain in the car trunk

November rain—
long ropes of the window washers
float in the wind

thunder
my woodshavings roll
along the veranda

vegetable stand
the owner sprinkling water
with a bunch of kale

heat of the day
still in the brick wall
of the liquor store

summer's end
the quickening of hammers
towards dusk

a dusting of snow
tire tracks grow visible
in the road's soft edge

after Christmas
a flock of sparrows
in the unsold trees

20,000 feet
traces of masking tape
on the jet engine

overnight bus
the young mother
sucks her thumb

how come
whatshisname
never speaks to me

his fury
pulled up short
by the payphone cord

I set the alarm
get out of bed to unpack
her photograph

with a flourish
the waitress leaves behind
rearranged smears

custody battle
a bodyguard lifts the child
to see the snow

how desirable
in the thrift store window
my old Mah-Jongg set

coming home weary
the broken tread announces
my floor is next

unexpected news
she stands staring into
the cutlery drawer

freshening breeze
the skillet softly chimes
against another

chill night
after you the toilet seat
slightly warm

The crow flies off . . .
    mountains fall away
      beneath him

Rowing
   out of the mist
      into the bright colors

At the river-bend
   wriggling towards the setting sun
      a lone watersnake

The lights are going out
   in the museum, a fetus
      suddenly darkens

The reflected door
   opens
      the mirror deepens

Winter dawn;
   from the deepest part of the forest
      crows are calling

Weight lifter
slowly lifting
the tea cup

Downpour
the palm reader
does her nails

Old retriever;
   he opens one eye
      at the tossed stick

After falling down
she asks for a bandaid
for her doll too

No matter
where I stand . . .
barbecue smoke

Snowflake's fall
into the darkness
of the tuba

I shut down the lawnmower
a call for supper
over the still grass

stripping wallpaper into the nite
my wife uncovers someone
else's bedroom

I hear her sew
I hear the rain
I turn back a page

first snow
lites our bedroom
she puts on the flowered sheets

for the smell
I plane another shaving
snow buries my tracks from the house

farm dog calling
calling to its echo
deep in the forest

bales of hay
dot the bluestem meadow—
morning breeze

a bike in the grass
one wheel slowly turning—
summer afternoon

rows of corn
stretch to the horizon—
sun on the thunderhead

pine shade
the wooden bench
worn smooth

mountain cherry—
from branch to branch
the photographer

two little boys
paddling like mad—
the beached canoe

wedding picture:
each face finds
a different camera

professional conference—
in the restroom all the dentists
washing their hands

candlelight dinner—
his finger slowly circles
the rim of his glass

rural interstate—
all the other cars
exit together

scenic overlook
the whole Mississippi valley
hidden in mist

fishermen's cars
parked along the road . . .
cold rain

exploring the cave . . .
   my son's flashlight beam
      disappears ahead

graduation day—
my son & I side by side
knotting our ties

summer sunset—
the baby finds his shadow
on the kitchen wall

silent prayer—
the quiet humming
of the ceiling fan

last bale of hay—
we sit down on it
and watch the moon

fresh scent . . .
the labrador's muzzle
deeper into snow

after
chickadee
stillness

the smell of the iron
as I come down the stairs
winter evening

from house
    to barn:
        the milky way

winter prairie—
a diesel locomotive
throttles down in the night

Deep within the stream
the huge fish lie motionless
facing the current.

A bitter morning:
  sparrows sitting together
    without any necks.

Searching on the wind,
  the hawk's cry . . .
    is the shape of its beak.

Half of the minnows
  within this sunlit shallow
    are not really there.

The fleeing sandpipers
  turn about suddenly
    and chase back the sea!

The stillness of dawn:
   crashing between the branches,
     a solitary leaf.

Wind gives way to calm
   and the stream smoothes, revealing
     its treasure of leaves.

Time after time
   caterpillar climbs this broken stem,
     then probes beyond.

An old spider web
   low above the forest floor,
     sagging full of seeds.

Wind sounds through the trees . . .
while here, gnats play in the calm
of wooded sunlight.

Indian summer:
   the scarecrow's jacket fades
      to a paler blue.

A pale dawn moon—
   furrows of the new-ploughed fields
      white with frost.

The time it takes—
   for snowflakes to whiten
      the distant pines.

After the snowfall . . .
   deep in the pine forest
     the sound of an axe.

Late snowfall;
   more and more yellow
      the forsythia.

Until it alights
   on a white daisy—just another
      blue dragonfly.

A hot summer wind—
   shadows of the windmill blades
      flow over the grass.

The sparkler goes out
   and with it—the face
      of the child.

On the old scarecrow
a crow sits for a while—
suddenly flies off.

winter rain
in our garage
the same stray cat

chained to the fence
the dog's collar

under the old car
oil puddles ripple
in the winter wind

on the padlock
snow
melting

in the mirror
the open door
blows shut behind me

clouds
blowing off the stars

broken bowl
the pieces
still rocking

wrinkles
in the white icing
of the birthday cake

grandmother's mirror—
age spots
the glass

bitter tea—
in the empty cup
the folded lemon

snowflakes—
dust on the toes
of my boots

pine needles
in the broken curve
of the ornament

closed bedroom door—
her shadow darkens
the crack of light

only letting in the cat
until
the morning star

first snow
brought in from the suburbs
on the neighbors' car

between lace curtains
the white cat's eyes
follow a snowflake

Sierra sunrise . . .
pine needles sinking deeper
in a patch of snow

cloud shadow
long enough
to close the poppies

returning quail
call to us from the moment
of which he speaks

soon after the child
                    the puppy
goes to sleep

while I'm gone
my dog
takes the driver's seat

children in single file
through the puddle
again

wet snow—
another color or two
on the sycamore boughs

a robin listens
     then flies off
          snow eddies

this spring rain
the thief too
curses his job

Holding the water,
     held by it—
          the dark mud.

writing again
the tea water
boiled dry

I look up
from writing
to daylight.

summer moon—
the only white
in the afternoon sky

going over a bump
the car ahead
going over a bump

the fence post
hangs upright in the washout—
mid-summer heat

commercial break—
the cat and I
head for the kitchen

the red ribbon award
for my first sunflower
has faded to orange

rain splashing—
the waiting room door
closes

yesterday's paper
in the next seat—
the train picks up speed

rest stop—
in the darkness
the grass stiff with frost

one mirror for everyone
the rest stop
rest room

coffee
in a paper cup—
a long way from home

on the ceiling
a large leak stain—
autumn coolness

the library book
overdue—
slow falling snow

snow now rain—
your picture
by mine

no one moves—
the winter evening
darkens the room

trash day—
the garbage truck backs over
the new snow

home early—
your empty coat hanger
in the closet

stalled car.
foot tracks being filled
with snow.

sun & moon
in the same sky
the small hand of my wife

time to go—
the stones we threw
at the bottom of the ocean

the wind going away—
the tape measure pulled past
the numbers

late evening heat
the newspaper rattles
in the fan's breeze

morning fog
not seeing far
the fern's underside

waiting room quiet
            an apple core
    in the ashtray

unsnapping
the holster strap
summer heat

quietly
the fireworks
far away

distant thunder—
the dog's toenails click
against the linoleum

night comes—
picking up your shoes
still warm

up late—
the furnace comes on
by itself

my wife still asleep—
snow piles up
on the steps

letting
the dog out—
the stars out

morning quiet
snow sticking to this side
of the telephone poles

While the guests order,
  the table cloth hides his hands—
    counting his money.

Down from the bridge rail,
  floating from under the bridge,
    strangers exchange stares.

In that empty house,
  with broken windows rattling,
    a door slams and slams.

Leaves moil in the yard,
   reveal an eyeless doll's head . . .
      slowly conceal it.

In that lightning flash—
   through the night rain—I saw it!
      . . . whatever it was.

A Hallowe'en mask,
   floating face up in the ditch,
      slowly shakes its head.

Hair, in my comb's teeth,
   the color of autumn wind—
      this whole day is gray.

Last screech owl cry—
How quietly the dawnlight
comes creeping through the woods.

Thunder storm passing—
echoing along the shore
that last hollow sound . . .

This evening stillness . . .
just the rusted cowbell
found by the pasture gate.

Cliff dweller ruins
and the silence of swallows
encircling silence.

Somewhere behind me,
seeming in dark silence
to feel a slow coiling.

Where the coyote called,
rising in full cry, the moon . . .
the sound of silence.

That breeze brought it—
a moment of moonlight
to the hidden fern.

Fall wind in pinyons . . .
Faster and louder patters
    yesterday's shower.

Mountain shadow
crossing the evening river
at the old fording place.

Under ledges
and looking for the coolness
that keeps touching my face.

Finding this cavern—
following the lantern light . . .
followed by silence.

the boat sails
close-hauled to the breeze
windward pines

bright sun
the sheen of tall grass
when it bends

clouds seen
through clouds
seen through

calm evening
the ballgame play-by-play
across the water

ground fog
up to my ankles
in moonlight

In my medicine cabinet,
　　the winter fly
has died of old age.

Birds singing
　　in the dark
—Rainy dawn

Straining at the padlock,
　　the garage doors
At noon.

Evening coming—
    the office girl
Unloosing her scarf.

Arms folded
    to the moon,
Among the cows.

Missing a kick
    at the icebox door
It closed anyway.

raining . . .
a can of paint
holds open the door

rainy afternoon
car wash deserted

November snow
    garage door left gaping

fog . . .
just the tree and I
at the bus stop

home from a journey,
my reflection in the glass
of the front door

small box from japan
the smile of the clay buddha
through the packing straw

mounted butterflies
    snowflakes
    through the window

from winter storage
　　the prow of the canoe
　　　　entering sunlight

pausing
halfway up the stair—
white chrysanthemums

a plastic rose
rides the old car's antenna—
spring morning

leaving   all the morning glories   closed

the old album:
not recognizing at first
my own young face

the far shore
drifting out of the mist
to meet us

a lizard inching
with the shadow of the stone
nearer the cave's mouth

far back under a ledge
the ancient petroglyph   faint
water sound

still . . . some echo
the pale jade cricket box
in the museum

perfect summer sky—
one blue crayon
missing from the box

cleaning brushes . . .
the last ray of sun
drying the ink stone

first heat wave—
coolness
of the bike store's basement

a shower darkens—
in the summer bookstore
the smell of new novels

a screendoor's quiet
rain and the sound of spoons placed
carefully away

summer afternoon
　　a beach umbrella
　　no one comes to

Moonlit sleet
In the holes of my
Harmonica

At the bottom
Of the rocky mountain slope
A pile of pebbles

The longest night:
Only the snowman stares
At the stars

Quietly shaping
The hollow of the blossom
The morning sunrise

Wild rose bending—
And bending even more
With the bee's weight

Over dried grass,
Two butterflies—
And a chill wind . . .

Duck feathers
On the lake's shore
Silent skies

Summer stillness
the play of light and shadow
on the windchimes

A doe's leap
darkens the oyster shell road:
twilight

I shake the vase—
a bouquet of red roses
finds its shape

Moon
and melon cooling
with us in the stream

first frost . . .
on a silver card tray
wild persimmons

an icicle the moon drifting through it

snow by the window paper flowers gathering dust

thawing ice the garbage blooming out of it

the silence a droplet of water trickles down a stone

passing clouds only a stand of aspens is in light

alone tonight one fish ripples the lake

deep in my notebook a lily pad floats away

overtaken
  by a single cloud
    and letting it pass . . .

the bluebird alights
at once
on the bright wet twig

long summer day . . .
my neighbor's bull
at it again

letting my tongue
deeper into the cool
ripe tomato

peering out
the scarecrow's ear—
two glittering eyes

while we wait
to do it again,
the rains of spring

she leaves—
    warm pillow scent
    remaining

    twisting inland,
the sea fog takes awhile
    in the apple trees

a single tulip!
hopelessly,
i passed on

a poppy . . .
a field of poppies!
the hills blowing with poppies!

glimmering morning
silence unfolds all
the yucca

across the sands
the rippling quiet
cloud shadow

a side-canyon:
pausing a moment, listening
into its reach . . .

rowing downstream
red leaves   swirling
behind me

a small girl . . .
the shadows stroke
    and stroke her

the merry-go-round
as it turns
shines into the trees

look it's clear
to Saturn

hearing
    cockroach feet;
        the midnight snowfall

dead cat . . .
open-mouthed
to the pouring rain

the aging beauty
having her knee x-rayed
points her toe

every Sunday
the marlin leaping
  from father's necktie

small child
afraid to throw away
  his Church Bulletin

second husband
painting the fence
the same green

    hearing us argue,
our old dog tiptoes past
    her empty water bowl

the lights on the tree
before the plug goes in

old woman, wrapping
her cat's gifts
—centering the bows

    summer night
newly-weds cutting shelfpaper
    —their bright light

evening lecture
a shadow hangs
from the pointing finger

her silence at dinner
sediment
       hanging in the wine

crying
she moves deeper
into the mirror

with the last lamp
stripping
her shadow off

moonrise   white cat eating the cardinal

Summer noon;
the blueberry field divided
by a muddy road

silent deer   the sound of a waterfall

farther and farther
into the mountain trail
autumn dusk deepens

surrounding
the quiet bungalow
yellow crime scene tape

MARLENE MOUNTAIN

end of the cold spell
i'd forgotten the color
of my under socks

winter night writing letters to get letters

wood pile
on the sagging porch
unstacking itself

pig and i spring rain

empty mailbox
i pick wildflowers
on my way back

he leans on the gate going staying

a quiet day
an old man on his tractor
passes at dusk

on this cold
          spring   1
      2 night 3   4
      kittens
      wet
          5

o

g

r

f   frog

                                      stick
    my neighbor's rooster hops the   i throw

                          beneath
                          leaf mold
                            stone
                             cool
                            stone

early morning wind in the umbrella of the pumpkin stand

        old towel   folding it again   autumn evening

at dusk hot water from the hose

pick-up truck
guns on the window rack
  the heat

one fly everywhere the heat

summer night clothes whirling in a dryer

above the mountain mountains of the moon

faded flowers of the bed sheets autumn night

seed catalog in the mailbox   cold drizzle

acid rain less and less i am at one with nature*

*less and less nature is nature

old pond a frog rises belly up

first time out—
sled runners leaving
rust tracks in the snow

toy shop window
a tiny sleigh waits
at the doll house door

winter sunset—
long shadows follow us home
from the sledding hill

neighbor's children leave . . .
casually the cat slips out
of the hall closet

evening séance—
the medium's parlor
smells of cabbage

moonless winter night
beyond the last street lamp
breakers pound the beach

after tires
on the wet country road
pine-dripping silence

wheelruts
of the old logging road
flowing with rain

November evening—
raindrops blow from the pine
into the mist

empty verandah
of the old resort hotel—
rain drips from the eaves

inside
the hailstone
ripples on a pond

on the sandal I take off
a dew-covered slug
continues its journey

not a cloud in sight
I put the red flag up
on the mailbox

heaped
in the buttercup
blue sky

from the pinecone
one furry spider leg
then another

one by one
eyes close in the henhouse
stars appear

first cold night
the fat tomcat hangs from
the window screen

at the fruitstand
taking off my mitten
to feel the coconut

long winter night
I open the red cookie tin
for needle and thread

ALAN PIZZARELLI

light rain
on the young tree
a strip of burlap   flaps

on the peddler's truck
an emptied scale   swings
in the morning sunlight

a bright awning is cranked
over the corner fruitstand

the gas station man
    points the way
with a gas nozzle

on the bright marquee
a man's shadow changes the letters

reaching for
the wind-up toy
it rides off the table

driving
out of the car wash

clouds move
across the hood

bending back
along the railroad track
tiger lilies

tiny fish
swaying
into the current
shadows rippling
over a hubcap

carried from the car
the ventriloquist's dummy
looks around

squinting
to read the sign
"optician"

on the windswept corner
traces of a puddle
fade

done
the shoeshine boy
snaps his rag

a spark
falls to the ground
    darkens

that's it

tonite
nothing to write

but this

PORNO MOVIE

the girl
      loosens her bra
starts peeling off panties
      darkens

    25¢

just before dawn
a beachball   floats
across the stillness of the pool

lightens

the dog runs after the stick
i pretend to throw

buzzZ
    slaP
buzzZ

under the boardwalk
sunlight brightens and fades

flinging the frisbee
skips off the ground
    curving up   hits a tree

      petals

drop of ocean
in my navel
reflects
the amusement park

hottest day of the year
a breeze in the distant treetops

it's here!

on the boardwalk
high above the crowd
a man on stilts

the tattoo'd man
walks onto the crowded beach

   the bearded lady
  hangs her wash
against the wind

late in the evening
a midget hoses the sunflowers

the setting sun
lights the top
of the high striker

the fat lady
bends over the tomatoes
a full moon

the ferris wheel turning
into the fog

the taffy pullers
            the taffy pullers
the taffy pullers

on the merry-go-round
that empty blue bench

in the shadows of the trees
by the amusement park
a firefly

at shortstop
between innings
sparrows dust-bathing

october rain
the tarpaulin ripples
across the infield

game over
all the empty seats
turn to blue

twilight
staples rust
in the telephone pole

snow falls from trees
rumble
of passing boxcars

with no money
    i go
    snow viewing

sun brightens
snow   slides off
the car bumper

wiping the chrome
blue vapors fade

a few snowflakes
fall on the candy store window
the lights go out

starry night
the jeweler
closes the folding gate

putting away the sled
the frayed rope
drags in the mud

coming home
flower
       by
           flower

waiting for guests
  a corner of the rug
  keeps turning up

unpainted porch
  fog comes
  to a closed door

unable
        to get hibiscus red
the artist eats the flower

        piano practice
through an open window
        the lilac

buttoning his fly
the boy with honeysuckle
clenched in his mouth

        in white tulips
the rooster's red head
        flowering

brushing my sins
the muscatel breath
of the priest

the cat
lowers his ears
to the master's fart

after Beethoven
he gets the furnace
roaring

white orchid
on her coffin
     the pickle lady

tape
recording
mountain silence

   in the stream
stones making half
   the music

ordering my tombstone
the cutter has me feel
his Gothic "R"

the sailor
peeling potatoes
around himself

     pacing
the shore
    the ship's cat

flea . .
that you
Issa?

light
lights
light

downpour:
my "I-Thou"
T-shirt

swish of cow tail
    peach petals
    fall

leaving a bookmark
by Issa's wild goose—
    to pick wild strawberries

by the autumn hill
my watercolor box
unopened

birthcry!
        the stars
        are all in place

seance
a white
moth

campfire extinguished,
the woman washing dishes
in a pan of stars

he removes his glove
        to point out
                        Orion

snow
all's
new

icy dawn . . .
the sparkling window frost
in the unused room

morning train—
its shadow moves across
a bank of snow

silence
the snow-covered rock
under winter stars

Thoreau's gravesite:
the smell of woodsmoke
on the cold spring air

Sunday morning:
pale violet lilacs behind
the old library

sunny afternoon
all the fire engines gone from
the open bays

Smelling faintly
of roses
the morning mist.

Cabbage moth—
the whole golf course
to itself.

Yachts all docked—
the tinkle
of ice.

At the top
of the ferris wheel,
lilac scent.

Lying—
I tell him I'm not looking
for a prince.

Among morning-glories
the drip drip
of lingerie.

Sunset:
riding the merry-go-round
alone.

Deep
in the inkwell
a star.

Undressed—
today's role dangles
from a metal hanger.

Just friends:
he watches my gauze dress
blowing on the line.

starrynightIenteryourmirror

With wine glasses
we stand and talk
into the rhododendrons.

His footsteps in the room
above me: slowly
I brush my hair.

Late August
I bring him the garden
in my skirt.

Waterlilies . . .
in a moment he'll ask me
what I'm thinking.

In his wedding band watching the clouds pass.

Leading him in . . .
my bracelet
jangling.

Lying in the wet grass,
him still beating
inside me.

Against his coat
I brush my lips—
the silence of snowflakes.

Only I laugh
at his joke . . .
the silence.

After an affair
sweeping
all the rooms.

Trying to forget him
stabbing
the potatoes.

In the garbage bin
mound of snow
and a valentine.

Opening his
dresser drawer—
darkness slips out.

Clutching a fist of hair
from my brush
I watch him sleep.

Discussing divorce
he strokes
the lace tablecloth.

During our argument
a pink rose
tightens its petals.

In the guest room
where my mother slept
I look for comfort.

Sitting together on the stoop,
the dog's hip
presses mine.

Summer afternoon:
the smell
of inner tubes.

Surrendering to a rain-washed stone.

Moving with
the clock-tower's shadow
the flower lady.

Vase of peonies:
on a white bud
lipstick print.

A butterfly lands on Park Place.

Chin on the broom   floating petals.

She's running for office—
for the first time
my neighbor waves.

300 miles away—
my father makes sure
I hear him sigh.

My last day at work—
already someone has taken
the stapler from my desk.

After the atheist's sneeze
I bite
my tongue.

Quickly I powder my nose
my mother
staring back.

Snow on the graves—
the sound
of a distant plane.

Asleep among
Christmas ribbons
the cats.

Winter morning—
the sound of eggs boiling
in an enamel pot.

Christmas cookies—
nibbling
stars.

From her neon window
the crystal gazer
stares into winter rain.

In the passing caboose   Christmas lights.

warehouse-theatre's
muffled cries the
soft night rain

red-flashing lights
on the leaves by the window—
they draw down the shade

winter drizzle . . .
the street-preacher's heels
   rise from the box

walk's end . . .
   the cold of his hand
    shook mine

bolted   space

the lights on the corners
click and change

held it,
a peony
    —black Rolls

Moving
   through the criteria—
         a breeze.

sparrows sunning
on the slaughterhouse

terminal.
one far off and
perfect moon

the long night
of the mannequins—
snow falling

warm spring day
in the empty classroom
a forgotten book

driving to work
past the woods
and the wild roses

between cities
on the interstate
so many stars

ever since I was a child
the moon
following me home

no moon tonight
our eyes are drawn
to the white chrysanthemum

the men on both sides
have taken
my armrests

the haiku
completely gone
by the time I've dried my hands

stocking feet
the width of each board
down the long hallway

androgynous stranger
winks at me

horror movie
commercial break
my son follows me into the kitchen

after lights out
the cat
finding things to do

Across the still lake
   through upcurls of morning mist—
     the cry of a loon

Mirrored by the spring
   under the pines, a cluster
    of Indian-pipes

A patter of rain...
   The lily-pad undulates
    on widening rings

Perching bolt upright—
   the crow lets the rain-water
    trickle from her tail

Down to dark leaf-mold
  the falling dogwood-petal
    carries its moonlight

Now the leaves are still—
  and only the mockingbird
    lets the moonlight through!

In the garden pool,
  dark and still, a stepping-stone
    releases the moon

The old rooster crows...
  Out of the mist come the rocks
    and the twisted pine

The waves now fall short
of the stranded jellyfish...
In it shines the sky

This morning's rainbow
   shares its deep violet edge
      with the misty moon

One breaker crashes...
   As the next draws up, a lull—
      and sandpiper-cries

In the sea, sunset...
   On the dark dune, a bright fringe
      of waving grasses

Hushed, the lake-shore's pines...
   Once more a steady mountain
     rests on steady clouds

Still sunlit, one tree...
   Into the mountain-shadow
     it lets fall a leaf

Snow-laden bushes—
   one bent to the ground, and one
     swaying in the wind

On the top fence-rail
   she lights, knocking off some snow—
     a common sparrow

At the window, sleet...
Here in the darkening hut—
sudden squeaks of mice

Blue jays in the pines;
the northern river's ledges
cased with melting ice

Tar paper cabin
  behind the river's white birch
    —a muskellunge leaps

Patches of snow
  mirrored in the flowing stream;
    a long wedge of geese

Marsh marigold
  on a low island of grass;
    the warmth of the sun

Muttering thunder . . .
the bottom of the river
scattered with clams

A light river wind;
   on the crannied cliff
      hang harebell and fern

Shooting the rapids!
   —a glimpse of a meadow
      gold with buttercups

Lean-to of tin;
   a pintail on the river
      in the pelting rain

A dirt road . . .
   acres of potato plants
      white-flowered under the moon

Asparagus bed
   silent in the morning mist
      the wild turkeys

Dry, summer day;
   chalk-white plover mute
      on a mid-stream rock

Ostrich fern on shore;
   a short-eared owl in an oak
      watching the canoe

Becoming dusk,—
    the catfish on the stringer
    swims up and down

Wispy autumn clouds;
   in the river shallows
     the droppings of a deer

A long wedge of geese;
   straw-gold needles of the larch
     on the flowing stream

Winter wind—
   bit by bit the swallow's nest
     crumbles in the barn

The chain saw stops;
   deeper in the winter woods
     a chickadee calls

Winter moon;
   a beaver lodge in the marsh,
      mounded with snow

cold saturday—
drawn back into bed
by my own warmth

too quick to reply
cutting my tongue
on the envelope

under the
blackest doodle
something unerasable

bouncing along
on the guardrails
car shadow

checking the driver
as I pass a car
just like mine

tourist town
postcards of the waterfall
racked upside down

deliberations
on a charge of murder
turning spring outside

the river always
out there in the dark
late train home

moon breaks over the hill
a dreaming driver
dims his brights

winter solstice
sheen of the cherry's bark
streaked with rain

tarp slapping—
the fragrance of lumber
in the winter mist

yellow iris buds . . .
on the back of his sketch pad,
the pond's reflection

wind dying down:
   from a mossy rockface
     the faintest trickle

lighting the path
to Walden Pond—
   my bedside lamp

alone at last
i wonder where
everyone is

Fresh snow at dawn
already the footsteps
of the neighbor's cat

becoming a photograph   winter afternoon

A sigh from her
then one from me—
two pages turn

Swinging on the hanger
her white summer dress:
wind chimes

Night begins to gather   between her breasts

Sunrise:
I forget my side
of the argument

Unhappy wife
I pedal my bike
through puddles

On the bus
the teenager pulls out a mirror
and adjusts her pout

Spring morning   gravedigger whistling

stars   crickets

In the town dump I find a still-beating heart

Street violinist
   fallen leaves
      in the open case

One button undone
in the clerk's blouse—I let her
steal my change

One by one to the floor   all of her shadows

Leaving my loneliness   inside her

At dawn   remembering her bad grammar

On the face
that last night called me names—
morning sunbeam

Windless summer day:
the gentle tug of the current
on the fishing pole

Summer night:
in my eyes starlight
hundreds of years old

Long train
horizon sun flickers through
the empty cattle cars

Evening shadows
fill the autumn market—
the unsold duck quacks

Deep snow
following in my footsteps
winter twilight

The frozen breaths
of the carolers   disappearing
among the stars

Mental hospital   my shadow stays outside

At the end of myself   pencil tip

Passport check:
my shadow waits
across the border

After the search for meaning   bills in the mail

At the edge of the precipice   I become logical

Thick fog lifts—
unfortunately, I am where
I thought I was

dewy morning:
the logging truck's load
sweating sap

trembling in the steady rain
     caterpillar tents
in the crabapple

leaning into the coolness
the flat tops of Queen Anne's lace
gleam with rain

thunder rumbles in the distance
     drenched kitchen screens dry
mesh by mesh

mist lifts from the hills
    wet barn wood
steams

tugging the snarl
out of its chain—
neighbor's watchdog

walking into and out of
    the sound
of the brook

a white mare grazes
in a grove of birch
thunderheads

row after row of radishes
    each top shivering
in the cool rain

the flatbed of baled hay
rocks with the tractor's pull
Indian summer

windy mountain summit—
　　the warmth of the sun
on my rippling jacket

an old road through the hills
　　fallen leaves
fill the potholes

far into twilight
milkweed crosses the meadow
the evening star

As day breaks . . .
   the lightness of her breath
      on my back

A wisp of spring cloud
   drifting apart from the rest . . .
      slowly evaporates

Sitting in the sun
   in the middle of the plants
      that I just watered

In an autumn wind,
   looking through a box of books
      left on the corner

After gazing at stars . . .
   now, I adjust to the rocks
      under my sleeping bag

Without a trail . . .
   the silence of snow falling
    around the mountain

End of a windy day . . .
   the last light lingers
    among the pampas plumes

In the snow
around the carousel
tracks of a horse

White lilac scent—
   the dollhouse at the window
     with its window open

Left open wide
   at the centre
     the butterfly book

Motionless
   a thousand feet above the hummingbird
     the condor's wings

Staring at me
   from the roar of the river
     a wild horse

Autumn colors
  breaking through the haze
    the wood duck settles

With me the same cloud   out of the covered bridge

october loneliness
two walking sticks

Colouring itself across the pond the autumn wind

Owl feather
  in my palm
    —the feel of moonlight

lingering snow
the game of catch continues
into evening

changing pitchers
the runner on first looks up
at a passing cloud

the batter checks
the placement of his feet
"Strike One!"

summer afternoon
the long fly ball to center field
takes its time

slow inning
the right fielder is playing
with a dog

after the game
a full moon rises over
the left field fence

from behind me
the shadow of the ticket-taker
comes down the aisle

lonely night
the faces painted on the windows
of a toy bus

the blues singer
tells how bad it is
then the sax tells you too

in the mirrors on her dress
little pieces of my
self

through the small holes
in the mailbox
sunlight on a blue stamp

the evening paper
on the darkening lawn
first star

a letter stuck
in the 11th floor mail chute
summer night

end of the line
the conductor starts turning
the seats around

the shadow in the folded napkin

a branch
waves in the window
and is gone

autumn twilight—
in the closed barbershop
the mirrors darken

raining at every window

November evening
the wind from a passing truck
ripples a roadside puddle

snow drifts
above the bear's den
starry night

spring breeze
the woods road is still wet
under the pines

hot day
a rock caught on a ledge
in the waterfall

stillness
sand sifts through the roots
of a fallen tree

late autumn
the great rock reappears
in the woods

a stick goes over the falls at sunset

as the sun comes out
a sail appears from behind
the island

reading a mystery
a cool breeze comes through
the beach roses

starting to rise
to the top of the wave
the duck dives into it

summer afternoon
the coolness of the newspaper
from the grocery bag

a tidepool
in a clam shell
the evening sunlight

shading his eyes
the wooden Indian looks out
at the spring rain

the sun goes down
my shovel strikes a spark
from the dark earth

the geese have gone—
in the chilly twilight
empty milkweed pods

late autumn—
sunlight fades from a sandbank
deep in the woods

snowstorm
a baseball glove
under the Christmas tree

the slow day . . .
in the empty motel corridor
a stack of dirty dishes

The first hot night:
chilling the tea
slicing the lemons.

hot afternoon . . .
only the slap slap
of a jump rope

behind sunglasses
I doze and wake . . .
the friendly man talks on

the swan's head
turns away from sunset
to his dark side

Quiet afternoon:
water shadows
on the pine bark.

mullein
with nothing around it
but the air

low tide:
all the people
stoop

on the hot lawn
only the mushroom's
shade

rustling beneath
the leaf cover, I pluck
the bean cool

trickling
over the dam—
summer's end

red flipped out
chicken lung
in a cold white sink

Emerging hot and rosy
from their skins—
beets!

my spade turns
the dark earth   lets in
some sun

all morning
the vegetable garden shaded
autumn

quiet evening:
   the long sound
      of the freight train fades

snowflakes begin . . .
at the cellar window
the red geranium blooms

Awakening . . .
the cold fresh scent:
new snow.

following me
deeper into my quilt
the wren's song

I sigh
and the cat on my lap
begins to purr

at the end
of the coal train's sound
winter dawn

walking the snow-crust
       not sinking
          sinking

Darkening
the cat's eyes:
a small chirp.

morning bath
clouds & birds float between
still wet limbs

spring breeze . . .
   her breasts sway
over the porcelain tub

she turns the child
to brush her hair
with the wind

holding you
in me still . . .
sparrow songs

twilight
taking
the trees

the dark
throbbing
with spring
peepers

no sound to this
spring rain—
but the rocks darken

Claiming
the outhouse roof:
peacock!

not seeing
the room is white
until that red apple

spring twilight . . .
    the hanging fern
        turns

a phoebe's cry . . .
the blue shadows
on the dinner plates

lily:
out of the water . . .
out of itself

over spatterdocks,
turning at corners of air:
dragonfly

heat before the storm:
a fly disturbs the quiet
of the empty store

bass
picking bugs
off the moon

approaching autumn:
the warehouse watchdog's bark
weakens in the wind

Thanksgiving alone:
ordering eggs and toast
in an undertone

town barberpole
stops turning:
autumn nightfall

the first snowfall:
down the cellar staircase
my father calls

New Year's Eve:
pay phone receiver
dangling

the blind musician
extending an old tin cup
collects a snowflake

Easter morning . . .
the sermon is taking the shape
of her neighbor's hat

my spring love affair:
the old upright Remington
wears a new ribbon

lone red-winged blackbird
riding a reed in high tide—
billowing clouds

the junkyard dog
in the shadow of the shack:
the heat

taking a hard look
at myself from all angles—
the men's store mirrors

removing
the bullet-proof vest:
the heat

the cathedral bell
is shaking a few snowflakes
from the morning air

barking its breath
into the rat-hole:
bitter cold

a crow in the snowy pine . . .
inching up a branch,
letting the evening sun through

winter evening
leaving father's footprints:
I sink into deep snow

the sack of kittens
sinking in the icy creek,
increases the cold

deep in rank grass,
through a bullet-riddled helmet:
an unknown flower

—*In memory of Lawrence J. Virgilio*

the autumn wind
has torn the telegram and more
from mother's hand

flag-covered coffin:
the shadow of the bugler
slips into the grave

my gold star mother
and father hold each other
and the folded flag

Viet Nam monument
darkened by the autumn rain:
my dead brother's name

my dead brother . . .
hearing his laugh
in my laughter

another autumn
still silent in his closet:
father's violin

on the darkened wall
of my brother's bedroom:
the dates and how tall

the hinge of the year:
holding up candles in church
lighting up our breaths

my palsied mother,
pressing my forehead on hers
this Ash Wednesday

my dead brother . . .
wearing his gloves and boots:
I step into deep snow

sixteenth autumn since:
barely visible grease marks
where he parked his car

after father's wake
the long walk in the moonlight
to the darkened house

into the blinding sun . . .
the funeral procession's
glaring headlights

at the open grave
mingling with the priest's prayer:
honking of wild geese

adding father's name
to the family tombstone
with room for my own

on my last journey
alone on the road at dawn:
first sight of the sea

autumn twilight:
the wreath on the door
lifts in the wind

landing swallow—
the ship's chain
dips slightly

spring breeze through the window . . .
stains on an apron
left at the counter

morning bird song—
my paddle slips
into its reflection

mountain spring—
in my cupped hand
pine needles

beach parking lot—
where the car door opened
a small pile of sand

low summer sun—
the shadow of an earring
on your cheek

after the quake
adding I love you
to a letter

fresh snow on the mat—
the shape of welcome
still visible

after-dinner mints
passed around the table
. . . slow-falling snow

toll booth lit for Christmas—
from my hand to hers
warm change

spring breeze—
the pull of her hand
as we near the pet store

my face dripping . . .
the floppy-foot clown's
plastic flower

after the quake
  the weathervane
    pointing to earth

first day of summer
a postman delivers mail
in a safari hat

grocery shopping—
pushing my cart faster
through feminine protection

reading in bed
  my pulse flickering
  the lightly held bookmark

first snow . . .
the children's hangers
clatter in the closet

taking invisible tickets
at the foot of the basement stairs—
child's magic show

paper route
    knocking a row of icicles
    from the eave

home for Christmas:
my childhood desk drawer
empty

scouring pans—
snow deepening
in the yard

dreaming . . .
dust
on the window

wind:
the long hairs
on my neck

fly
on the flank
of the bronze horse

crickets . . .
then
thunder

first morning . . .
over the snow, a washing
steams on the line

the mirror fogs,
a name written long ago
faintly reappears

axe in the sun
wood-chips falling
cool on my skin

a road all puddles
        last light
on the woodcock's beak

Breathing . . .
     the teacup
fills with shadow

May rain . . .
On the sill, a feather
        shifts in the draught

A small noise . . .
papers uncrumpling.
        stillness again

trilliums rippling . . .
under her scarf
her pulse

I find her huddled on the bed
the paperback
closing by itself

away from eyes
the stairwell holds
us in its arms

bathing, I think of you
and lift the straw blind
to the rain

A page of Shelley
brightens and dims
        with passing clouds

weak sun
silverware dries cold
under the open window

cheeses, pâté
my mouth suddenly dry
when she looks at him

just her look
escapes from between her children
beach in fog

humiliated again
bar-smoke in the sweater
I pull from my head

can this be all?
just light
appears through the envelope

a game of solitaire—
    sun off the cards
  slashes at the walls

parked near her house.
a match flares
on the empty porch

what was I thinking?
toes suddenly cool
in river clay

mail on the counter
sits unopened
afternoon sun through birches

novel's end
on the cluttered desk
a pool of clear wood

musty shed
winter light
on the overturned canoe

Listening . . .
After a while,
  I take up my axe again

the dawn wind
fluffs the feathers
on the owl's neck

cold morning
a flock of crows settles
in distant trees

far out
a lone duck bobs and bobs . . .
the lake in winter

spring rain
the rocks in the garden
have settled

abandoned barn . . .
the faintest neighing
of horses

supper done . . .
the old folks sit
on the porch

autumn wind . . .
the rise and fall
of sparrows

sugar maple
the drawing class seated
before it

goats on the roof
of the chicken shack
spring morning

laurel in bloom
she lingers awhile
at the mirror

spring thaw
white horse in the pasture
nosing clouds

my hand moves out
touches the sun
on a log

the old cow lags
to loll and splash
spring evening

boulders
just beneath the boat
it's dawn

a marsh hawk
tips the solitary
pine

water pools
among the rocks   then pools
and pools again

a bluegill rises
to the match   wavers
and falls away

the moon at dawn
lily pads blow white
in a sudden breeze

a bluejay sails
to the bough of a pine
the coolness

a bittern booms
in the silence that follows
smell of the marsh

rain in gusts
below the deadhead
troutswirl

the hills
release the summer clouds
one   by one   by one

a stagnant pond
red dragonflies
the heat

water lilies
slithering through them
a leech

beyond the porch
the summer night   leaning out
a moment

the sun lights up a distant ridge   another

a mourning cloak
comes sailing down
the deerpath

along the gravel
speckled trout   their shadows
out before them

looking deeper
and deeper into it
the great beech

coolness
hemlock shadows flicker
across the boulder

i catch
the maple leaf   then let
it go

the day wears on
the logcock keeps on
drumming

dusk   from rock to rock a waterthrush

a pebble falls
bushes at the water's edge
just faintly glimmer

den of the bear
beyond the great rocks
storm clouds

the evening sun
slips over the log   follows me
downriver

another bend
now   at last   the moon
and all the stars

november evening
the faintest tick of snow
upon the cornstalks

in an upstairs room
of the abandoned house
a doll moongazing

deep winter . . .
all day long the mountainside
in shadow

a box of nails
on the shelf of the shed
the cold

mist for miles
through it runs the light
of a night train

morning meadow—
a wren follows
the sunshine in

clouds roll in—
the flow of silt down
the dry creek bed

snowmelt
a space opens
around the rock

light spring rain
the sound of an airplane
circling above the clouds

gathering light . . .
  one swell of the sea
becomes another

light
up under the gull's wing:
sunrise

flash on the rim—
side canyon prolonging
thunder

after the garden party   the garden

first cool evening
between the cricket chirps
the longer silence

sunrise path:
at each step the baby's shadow
releases her foot

the baby's pee
pulls roadside dust
into rolling beads

hot rock by the stream
each of the baby's toeprints
evaporating

warm rain before dawn:
my milk flows into her
unseen

picking the last pears
yellow windows hang
in the dusk

reunion:
a pause
before each hug

before the sled moves
the little girls already
squealing

windblown Christmas lights—
still place
between stars

On the first day of spring
snow falling
from one bough to another

In a circle of thaw
　the cat walks
　　round and round

violets
in a broken sac of dew—
the hoof of a deer

persimmons
lightly swaying—
    heavy with
    themselves

fallen birch leaf
  vein-side
    to the sky

The silence
in moonlight
of stones

The calliope!
    Walking to the fair
      a little faster.

Unable to decide
    which balloon to pick
      she begins to cry.

Still trembling
    after the Cyclone rumbles past:
      a row of Kewpie dolls.

Sprinkling again!
   A sulky driver lights up
      another cigar.

In the puddle
   another raindrop
      jiggles the fun house.

A frost at the fair.
   Steam rising in the moonlight
      from a mound of hay.

Falling from a horse
   in the carousel
      the morning dew.

Under a withered iris
   in the noon heat
      a crisp, blue ribbon.

In the French fry stand
   the World Series is turned down
      to hear her order.

Sulky drivers cracking their whips!
   A moth flutters up
      higher and higher.

The high diver
takes off her cape
in the stars.

Right in the middle
of the cat's yawn—
a pink tongue.

Opening its eyes
  closing its eyes
    a cat in the sun.

After a hard rain,
  a cat stops to shake a paw
    before moving on.

Following the smoke ring
  out the window
    the cat's eye.

Hopping over the mound
  and into the dugout—
    the first robin.

In the shade
  under a leaf
    a forked tongue.

Hard climb
  turning to look back
    more frequently now.

I stop to listen;
the cricket
has done the same.

THE HAIKU SOCIETY OF AMERICA DEFINITIONS

The following definitions were completed in 1973 by the HSA Committee on Definitions: Harold G. Henderson, William J. Higginson, and Anita Virgil. They were slightly revised in 1990 by Higginson and Virgil.

1. Though it was our original intention to confine ourselves to the discussion of haiku, we found it impossible to do this adequately without also covering the terms haikai, hokku, and senryu. By use of cross-referencing, we hope that we have been able to present a clear picture of the meaning of haiku in the briefest manner possible.

2. The Japanese words *jion* (symbol-sound) and *onji* (sound-symbol) have been mistranslated into English as

"syllable" for many years. However, in most Japanese poetry the *jion* or *onji* does not correspond to the Western notion of the syllable. For example, while each of the entry words is reckoned as two syllables in English, "hokku" and "haiku" are each counted as three *onji*, while "haikai" and "senryu" each have four *onji*. On the other hand, where each Japanese *onji* is equal and brief as "do, re, mi, etc.," English syllables can vary greatly in time duration. (For a further discussion of the Japanese sound system, see Roy Andrew Miller *The Japanese Language*.)

3. Each of the four entry words is its own plural.

HAIKU

(1) An unrhymed Japanese poem recording the essence of a moment keenly perceived, in which Nature is linked to human nature. It usually consists of seventeen *onji* (Japanese sound-symbols).

(2) A foreign adaptation of (1). It is usually written in three lines of fewer than seventeen syllables. (See also HAIKAI, HOKKU.)

NOTE to (2):

That part of the definition that begins "It is usually written" places a heavy weight on the word "usually." We depend on that word to provide latitude for variations to the syllable count and to the number of lines or other external aspects of "form" *providing* they meet the primary stringent requirements expressed in the first part of the definition. Rarely is a haiku longer than seventeen syllables.

While all Japanese classical haiku, as well as most modern

ones, contain a *kigo* (season-word: a word or phrase indicating one of the four seasons of their year), extreme variations of climate in the United States make it impossible to put a codified "season-word" into every American haiku. Instead, American adaptations include some reference to Nature within them.

HOKKU

(1) The first stanza of a Japanese linked-verse poem (see HAIKAI).

(2) (Obsolete) A haiku.

NOTE to (2):

Hokku was used as a synonym for haiku by the Imagist poets, but is obsolete in modern American usage. It is definitely obsolete today in Japan.

SENRYU

(1) A Japanese poem structurally similar to the Japanese haiku (which see), but primarily concerned with human nature. It is usually humorous or satiric.

(2) A foreign adaptation of (1).

HAIKAI

(1) A type of Japanese linked-verse poem, popular from the fifteenth through the nineteenth centuries. Such a poem normally consists of thirty-six, fifty, or one hundred stanzas, alternating seventeen and fourteen *onji* (Japanese

sound-symbols). Usually a small group of poets took turns composing the poem's stanzas, whose content and grammar were governed by fairly complex rules.

NOTES:

In Japanese, the word *haikai* is commonly used as an abbreviation for the phrase *haikai no renga*, usually translated as "comic linked-verse." Under the influence of Bashō (1644–1694), the tone of *haikai no renga* became more serious, but the name was retained. The word *haikai* is also used in Japanese as a general term for all haiku-related literature (haiku, *haikai no renga*, the diaries of haiku poets, etc.).

In Spanish and French the word *haikai* is often used to refer to either the Japanese haiku or Western adaptations of the Japanese haiku. However, in modern Japanese usage, reference to a single *haikai* is to a *haikai no renga*.

BIOGRAPHICAL NOTES

The following brief biographical entries include the state, province, or country where the poet currently resides, date and place of birth, and most recent book. For addresses of the haiku presses—AHA Books, Brooks Books, Burnt Lake, From Here, High/Coo, King's Road, Red Moon, and some others—see the Book List that follows the Foreword.

Eric Amann: Ontario; 1938 Munich, Germany; *Cicada Voices: Selected Haiku of Eric Amann 1966–1979*, edited by George Swede, High/Coo Press, 1983.

Kay M. Avila (also known as Kat Avila): California; 3/24/1958 Yokosuka, Japan; listed compiler of father's *Mexican Ghost Tales of the Southwest* by Alfred Avila, Arte Público Press, University of Houston, 1994.

Nick Avis: Newfoundland; 1/7/1957 London, England;

Footprints, King's Road Press, 1994.

Winona Baker: British Columbia; 3/18/1924 Southey, Saskatchewan; *Beyond the Lighthouse*, Oolichan Press, 1992.

Geri Barton: New York; 2/3/1927 Bronx, NY; in *Haiku World* by William J. Higginson, Kodansha International, 1996.

Mykel Board: New York; 1/31/1950 Long Island, NY; in *In the Waterfall*, Spring Street Haiku Group, 1997.

Bob Boldman: Ohio; 6/22/1950 Dayton, OH; *Heart and Bones*, Wind Chimes Press, 1985.

Miriam Borne: New York; 7/6/1946 Los Angeles (Venice Beach), CA; in *In the Waterfall*, Spring Street Haiku Group, 1997.

Jim Boyd: Virginia; 9/24/1944 San Mateo, CA; *one breath poems*, self-published, 1992.

Chuck Brickley: British Columbia; 10/11/1947 San Francisco, CA; *Earthshine*, unpublished.

David Burleigh: Japan; 6/27/1950 N. Ireland, UK; *Octopus Dreams*, privately published, 1998.

Jack Cain: Ontario; 12/16/1940 Newmarket, Ontario.

James Chessing: California; 8/21/1952 San Francisco, CA.

Margaret Chula: Oregon; 10/10/1947 Northfield, MA; *Always Filling, Always Full*, Katsura Press, due 1999.

Tom Clausen: New York; 8/1/1951 Ithaca, NY; *A Work of Love*, Tiny Poems Press, 1997.

Ellen Compton: Washington, DC; 4/3/1936 Wheeling, WV.

Gerard John Conforti: New York; 2/26/1948 New York, NY; *Now That the Night Ends*, AHA Books and Chant Press, 1996.

L. A. Davidson: New York; 7/31/1917 Near Roy, MT; *The Shape of the Tree*, Wind Chimes Press, 1982 (reprinted 1991, 1996).

Raffael de Gruttola: Massachusetts; 5/15/1935 Cambridge, MA.

Bruce Detrick: New York; 7/20/1941 Los Angeles, CA; in *1997 Red Moon Anthology*, Red Moon Press, 1998.

Mike Dillon: Washington; 5/29/1950 Seattle, WA.

Betty Drevniok: last resided Ontario; 12/17/1919 St. Louis, MO (d. 1997); *Thoughts of Spring*, King's Road Press, 1993.

Bernard Lionel Einbond: last resided New York; 5/19/1937 New York, NY (d. 1998).

David Elliott: Pennsylvania; 12/26/1944 Minneapolis, MN; *Wind in the Trees*, AHA Books, 1992.

Robert Epstein: California; 4/8/1954 New York, NY.

Judson Evans: Massachusetts; 4/30/1955 Wilkes-Barre, PA; in *Journeys to the Interior* (Haibun), edited by Bruce Ross, Charles E. Tuttle Company, 1998.

Dee Evetts: New York; 5/16/1943 Ware, England; *endgrain*, Red Moon Press, 1997.

Larry Gates: Mississippi; 6/12/1942 Chicago, IL.

Garry Gay: California; 3/28/1951 Glendale, CA; *Wings of Moonlight*, Smythe-Waithe Press, 1993.

LeRoy Gorman: Ontario; 8/7/1949 Smiths Falls, Ontario; *nothing personal*, proof press, 1998.

Lee Gurga: Illinois; 7/28/1949 Chicago, IL; *Fresh Scent: Selected Haiku*, Brooks Books, 1998.

J. W. Hackett: California; 8/6/1929 Seattle, WA; *The Zen Haiku and Other Zen Poems of J. W. Hackett*, Japan

Publications, Tokyo, 1983. (See Book List for more information.)

Lorraine Ellis Harr: Oregon; 10/31/1912 Sullivan, IL; *SEVENTY-SEVENS: Pathways of the Dragonfly*.

Penny Harter: New Mexico; 4/9/1940 New York, NY; *Lizard Light: Poems from the Earth*, Sherman Asher Publishing, 1998.

Doris Heitmeyer: New York; 7/20/1929 St. Louis, MO; *The Way of the Hawk*, self-published chapbook, 1998.

Christopher Herold: California; 4/23/1948 Suffern, NY; *Voices of Stone*, Kanshiketsu Press, 1995/96/97.

Frank Higgins: Missouri; 1953 Kansas City, MO; *Eating Blowfish*, Raindust Press, 1996.

William J. Higginson: New Mexico; 12/17/1938 New York, NY; *Haiku World: An International Poetry Almanac*. Kodansha International, Tokyo, 1996.

Kam Holifield: New York; 12/13/1916 Honolulu, HI; *Workshop Poems*, Big Apple Publishing, 1989.

Gary Hotham: Maryland; 7/28/1950 Presque Isle, ME; *Footprints & Fingerprints*, Lilliput Review: Modest Proposal Chapbooks, 1998.

Clement Hoyt: last resided Texas; 5/14/1906 Houston, TX (d. 1970); *Storm of Stars*, The Green World, Baton Rouge, LA, 1976.

Foster Jewell: last resided Illinois; 7/21/1893 Grand Rapids, MI (d. 1984); *Exhaling Green*, Sangre de Cristo Press, Venice, CA, 1980.

Jim Kacian: Virginia; 7/26/1953 Worcester, MA; *Six Directions*, La Alameda Press, Albuquerque, NM, 1998.

Jack Kerouac: last resided Florida; 3/12/1922 Lowell, MA

(d. 1969); *Scattered Poems*, City Lights Books, San Francisco, CA, 1971.

M. Kettner: Washington; 5/11/1947 Grand Rapids, MI; *INFRARED, poems from another spectrum*, Juxta Press, 1998, second edition.

Jerry Kilbride: California; 2/25/1930 Denver, CO; *Heaton Farm Haiku,* Wind Chimes, 1983.

Elizabeth Searle Lamb: New Mexico; 1/22/1917 Topeka, KS; *Ripples Spreading Out: Poems for Bruce and Others,* Tiny Poems Press, 1997.

Evelyn Lang: New Hampshire; 11/26/1939 Rochester, NH; *Woodsmoke*, a work in progress.

Burnell Lippy: Vermont; 4/16/1944 Hanover, PA.

Geraldine Clinton Little: last resided New Jersey; 9/20/1924 Portstewart, Ireland (d. 1997); *Woman in a Special House*, Fithian Press, Santa Barbara, CA, 1997.

David Lloyd: New Jersey; 5/9/1930 Montclair, NJ; *Snowman*, The Rook Press, P.O. Box 144, Ruffsdale, PA 15679, 1978.

Peggy Willis Lyles: Georgia; 9/17/1939 Summerville, SC; *Still at the Edge*, Swamp Press, Oneonta, NY, 1980.

Matsuo Allard (previously: R. Clarence Matsuo-Allard): New Hampshire; 12/15/1949 Manchester, NH; *Bird Day Afternoon*, High/Coo Press, 1978.

Michael McClintock: California; 3/31/1950 Los Angeles, CA; *Solstice*, Seer Ox Press, South Pasadena, CA, 1997.

Carol Montgomery: Pennsylvania: 11/24/1938 Pittsburgh, PA; *Starting Something*, Los Hombres Press, 1992.

Scott Montgomery: Washington; 5/30/1951 Ithaca, NY; *Movements of Knowledge: The Role of Translation in the Making of Modern Science*, University of Chicago Press, due 1999.

Lenard D. Moore: North Carolina; 2/13/1958 Jacksonville, NC; *FOREVER HOME*, St. Andrews College Press, 1992.

Joanne Morcom: Alberta; 12/28/1955 Calgary, Alberta.

Marlene Mountain: Tennessee; 12/11/1939 Ada, OK; *nature talks back*, self-published, 1994.

Patricia Neubauer: Pennsylvania; 6/12/1922 Philadelphia, PA; *Foxes in the Garden*, Lantern Press, 1993.

Joe Nutt: Virginia; 9/12/1935 Cleveland, OH; *Kernals*, self-published, 1989.

Carl Patrick: New York; 7/2/1937 Houston, TX; in *In the Waterfall*, Spring Street Haiku Group, 1997.

Alan Pizzarelli: New Jersey; 1/12/1950 Newark, NJ; *The Windswept Corner*, Islet Books, due 1999.

Jane Reichhold: California; 1/18/1937 Lima, OH; *In the Presence*, AHA Books, 1998.

Raymond Roseliep: last resided Iowa; 8/11/1917 Farley, IA (d. 1983); *The Earth We Swing On*, haiku by Raymond Roseliep, photos by Cyril A. Reilly and Renée Travis Reilly, Winston Press, Minneapolis, MN, 1984. © 1984 by Cyril A. Reilly and Renée Travis Reilly and the estate of Raymond Roseliep, © renewed 1985 Daniel J. Rogers.

Bruce Ross: Vermont; 3/1/1945 Hamilton, Ontario; *Silence: Collected Haiku*, HMS Press, 1997; (ed.) *Journey to the Interior: American Versions of Haibun*, Charles E. Tuttle, 1998.

Alexis Rotella: California; 1/16/1947 Johnstown, PA; *Sassy*,

Tragg Publications, 1998.

Martin Shea: California; 7/1/1941 New York, NY; *Roses from the South* (play), International Readers Theatre, Blizzard Publishing, Canada, 1995.

George Skane: Massachusetts; 8/11/1949 Boston, MA.

Karen Sohne: New York; 1/3/1957 Staten Island, NY; *such moonlight*, self-published, 1995.

O. Mabson Southard: British Columbia; 11/29/1911 Cambridge, MA; *Marsh-grasses*, American Haiku Press, 1967.

Robert Spiess: Wisconsin; 10/16/1921 Milwaukee, WI; *Noddy*, Modern Haiku Press, 1997.

John Stevenson: New York: 10/9/1948 Ithaca, NY; *Something Unerasable*, self-published, 1996.

Ebba Story: California; 7/27/1952 Augusta, GA.

George Swede: Ontario; 11/20/1940 Riga, Latvia; *My Shadow Doing Something*, Tiny Poems Press, 1997.

Wally Swist: Massachusetts; 4/26/1953 New Haven, CT; *The White Rose*, Timberline Press, Fulton, MO, 1999.

Tom Tico: California; 5/15/1942 San Francisco, CA; *Spring Morning Sun*, Morris Publishing, 1998.

vincent tripi: California; 6/9/1941 Brooklyn, NY; *tribe: Further Meditations of a Haiku Poet*, Swamp Press, 1998.

Cor van den Heuvel: New York; 3/6/1931 Biddeford, ME; *Puddles*, Chant Press, 1990.

Anita Virgil: Virginia; 11/23/1931 Baltimore, MD; *PILOT*, Peaks Press, 1996.

Nicholas Virgilio: last resided New Jersey; 6/28/1928 Camden, NJ (d. 1989); *Selected Haiku*, co-published by Burnt Lake Press and Black Moss Press, 1988.

Michael Dylan Welch: California; 5/20/1962 Watford, England; *Footsteps in the Fog*, Press Here, Foster City, CA, 1994.

Larry Wiggin: last resided New Hampshire; 11/15/1919 Northfield, NH (d. 1973); *loose kites*, self-published broadside, 1973.

Rod Willmot: Quebec; 12/27/1948 Toronto, Ontario; *Sayings for the Invisible*, Black Moss Press, 1988.

John Wills: last resided Florida; 7/4/1921 Los Angeles, CA (d. 1993); *mountain*, S.E. Publishing, Qual-Tech, Ellenton, FL, 1993.

Jeff Witkin: Maryland; 2/11/1953 Washington, DC; *Beyond Where the Snow Falls*, Tiny Poems Press, 1997.

Ruth Yarrow: Washington; 9/15/1939 Camden, NJ; *A Journal for Reflections*, The Crossing Press, Freedom, CA, 1988.

Virginia Brady Young: Connecticut; New York, NY.

Arizona Zipper: Maine; The White Mountains.

ACKNOWLEDGMENTS

The editor thanks the following poets, magazines, and publishers for permission to print these poems:

(Abbreviations: AAH: *An Anthology of Haiku by People of the United States and Canada* [JAL Contest Winners 1988]; AH: *American Haiku*; AHA: AHA Books; BLP: Burnt Lake Press; BS: *Brussels Sprout*; CI: *Cicada*; DR: *Dragonfly*; FHP: From Here Press; FR: *Frogpond*; HC: *High/Coo;* HH: *Haiku Highlights;* HM: *Haiku Magazine*; HP: Haiku Poets of Northern California; HSA: Haiku Society of America, Inc.; HW: *Haiku West*; JAL: Japan Air Lines; KR: King's Road Press; M: *Mayfly*; MH: *Modern Haiku*; NWH: *New World Haiku*; SO: *Seer Ox*; PH: Press Here; SS: Spring Street Haiku Group Chapbooks; WC: *Wind Chimes*; WN: *Woodnotes*; 1/1: Vol. 1, No. 1. A "P" after a magazine's abbreviation indicates the press associated with it; if the address of a press is not mentioned below, it might be found in the Book List which appears after the Foreword.)

(Note: Every effort has been made to contact copyright holders; the editor would be pleased to hear from any copyright holders not acknowledged below.)

The Parakeet's Mirror, SS, copyright © 1993 by Mykel Board; by permission of the author.

Bob Boldman: "mirror" from WC 26, copyright © 1988 by Bob Boldman; "leaves" from CI 4/4, © CI 1980; "mist" from BS I/2, © 1981 by Alexis Rotella; "in the doll's" from MH XIII/1, copyright 1982 Robert Spiess; "in the heat" from WC 6, copyright © 1982 by Hal Roth; "face" from WC 7, copyright © 1983 by Hal Roth; "a moment" and "day darkens" from CI 5/1, © CI 1981; "in the temple" and "the priest" from *Walking with the River*, HCP, © 1980 by Bob Boldman; "touching" and "i end" from CI 5/4, © CI 1981; "a fin" from BS II/4, © copyright 1982 by Alexis Rotella; "JANUARY" from BS I/3, © 1981 BS; by permission of the author.

Miriam Borne: "long meeting" from *In the Waterfall*, SS, copyright © 1997 by Miriam Borne; by permission of the author.

Jim Boyd: "morning surf" from MH XXIV/1, © 1993 by Jim Boyd; by permission of the author.

Chuck Brickley: "sheet lightning," "the puppet," and "outside" from MH XIV/1, copyright 1983 Robert Spiess; "deserted" from FR V/3, © 1982 HSA; by permission of the author.

David Burleigh: "After washing up" from *Winter Sunlight*, copyright © 1993 by David Burleigh; by permission of the author.

Jack Cain: "someone's" from HM 3/2, copyright 1969 by Eric W. Amann; "waiting" and "an empty" from HM 3/4, copyright 1969 by Eric W. Amann; by permission of the author.

Bruce Detrick: "between the twirlers" from *In the Waterfall*, SS, copyright © 1997 by Bruce Detrick; by permission of the author.

Mike Dillon: "Spring afternoon" from MH XXV/2, © 1994 Mike Dillon; "The last kid" from MH XXVI/3, © 1995 Mike Dillon; "August night" from MH XXVI/1, © 1995 Mike Dillon; by permission of the author.

Betty Drevniok: "autumn night" and "a drift" from *Thoughts of Spring*, Kings Road Press, copyright © 1993 by Betty Drevniok; "Deep snow" and "Snow at dusk" from WC 5, © 1982 Betty Drevniok; by permission of Charles Drevniok.

Bernard Lionel Einbond: "the white of her neck" from HM 2/3, copyright 1968 by Eric W. Amann; "the thousand colors" from *dreams wander* (HSA Members Anthology), © 1994 by Bernard Lionel Einbond; "frog pond" from *An Anthology of Haiku by People of the U.S. and Canada* (JAL 1988 Contest Winners), Grand Prize Winner, © 1988 by Bernard Lionel Einbond; by permission of the author.

David Elliott: "Shielding" from MH XXII/2, copyright © 1991 by David Elliott; all other poems (3) from *Wind in the Trees*, AHA Books, copyright © 1992 by David Elliott; by permission of the author.

Robert Epstein: "long July" from WN 30, copyright © 1996 by Robert Epstein; "back from vacation" from FR XX/2, copyright © 1997 by Robert Epstein; by permission of the author.

Judson Evans: "November rain" from FR XVI/2, copyright © 1993 by Judson Evans; by permission of the author.

copyright © 1997 by Lee Gurga; "candlelight" from FR XIV/2, copyright © 1991 by Lee Gurga; "silent" from *South by Southeast* 4/2, copyright © 1997 by Lee Gurga; "the smell" from *A Mouse Pours Out*, HCP, copyright © 1988 by Lee Gurga; "from house" from *The Red Moon Anthology*, Red Moon Press, copyright © 1997 by Lee Gurga; all other poems (9) from *The Measure of Emptiness*, Press Here, copyright © 1991 by Lee Gurga; by permission of the author.

J. W. Hackett: all 10 poems from *The Zen Haiku and Other Zen Poems of J. W. Hackett*, Japan Publications, Tokyo, © 1983 in Japan by James W. Hackett; by permission of the author. (See Book List for more information.)

Lorraine Ellis Harr: "Indian" from HW 8/1, copyright 1974 by Leroy Kanterman; "A pale dawn" and "Late snowfall" from HM 5/1, © William J. Higginson 1971; "The time" from DR 11/1, copyright 1983 by Lorraine Ellis Harr; "After the snowfall" from *Snowflakes in the Wind*, copyright 1976 by Lorraine Ellis Harr; "Until it alights" from *Tombo: 226 Dragonfly Haiku*, copyright 1975 by Lorraine Ellis Harr; "A hot summer" from DR 1/3, copyright 1973 by Lorraine Ellis Harr; "The sparkler" from DR 2/3, copyright 1974 by Lorraine Ellis Harr; "On the old" from *Cats Crows Frogs & Scarecrows*, copyright 1975 by Lorraine Ellis Harr; by permission of the author.

Penny Harter: "winter rain," "under the old car," "on the padlock," and "only letting in the cat" from *The Orange Balloon*, FHP, copyright © 1980 Penny Harter; "chained," "snowflakes," and "closed bedroom door"

and "commercial break" previously unpublished; by permission of the author.

Kam Holifield: "the red ribbon award" from *After Lights Out*, SS, copyright © 1996 by Kam Holifield; by permission of the author.

Gary Hotham: "rain splashing" and "snow now" from *Pulling Out the Bent Nail*, WCP, copyright © 1988 by Gary Hotham; "yesterday's" from *As Far as the Light Goes*, Juniper, copyright © 1990 by Gary Hotham; "rest stop" from MH XIII/1, copyright © 1982 by Gary Hotham; "one mirror," "time," and "the wind" from *Before All the Leaves Are Gone*, Juniper, copyright © 1996 by Gary Hotham; "on the ceiling," "home," "waiting," and "quietly" from *Without the Mountains*, © Gary Hotham 1976; "no one" from MH XX/3, copyright © 1989 by Gary Hotham; "trash" from MH XXIX/1, copyright © 1998 by Gary Hotham; "sun" and "morning fog" from *The Fern's Underside*, © 1977 by Gary Hotham; "late" from MH XXV/2, copyright © 1994 by Gary Hotham; "unsnapping" from SO 4, copyright © 1976 by Michael McClintock; "my wife" from FR III/1, copyright © 1980 HSA; "morning quiet" from CI 3/1, © CI 1979; all other poems (6) from *Against the Linoleum*, Yiqralo Press, copyright © 1979 by Gary Hotham; by permission of the author.

Clement Hoyt: "While" from AH I, copyright © 1963 by James Bull; all other poems (6) from *Storm of Stars*, The Green World, Baton Rouge, LA, copyright © 1976 by Violet Hoyt; by permission of Esther Jean Hoyt.

copyright © 1989 by Jerry Kilbride; by permission of the author.

Elizabeth Searle Lamb: "pausing" from *in this blaze of sun*, FHP, copyright © 1975 by Elizabeth Searle Lamb; "leaving" and "the old album" from *39 Blossoms*, HCP, © 1982 by Elizabeth Searle Lamb; "the far shore" from DR 2/1, copyright 1974 by Lorraine Ellis Harr; "still" from MH X/3, copyright © 1979 by Robert Spiess; all other poems (3) from *Casting into a Cloud*, FHP, copyright © 1985 by Elizabeth Searle Lamb; by permission of the author.

Evelyn Lang: "perfect summer sky" from MH XXIV/3, copyright © 1993 by Evelyn Lang; "cleaning brushes" from *The Nor'Easter*, 1/2, copyright © 1993 by Evelyn Lang; by permission of the author.

Burnell Lippy: "first heat wave" from MH XXIX/1, copyright © 1998 by Burnell Lippy; "a shower" from MH XXVII/3, copyright © 1996 by Burnell Lippy; "a screendoor's" from MH XXVI/2, copyright © 1995 by Burnell Lippy; by permission of the author.

Geraldine Clinton Little: "summer afternoon" from FR VIII/3; copyright © 1985 by Geraldine Clinton Little; by permission of Rory Little and Tim Little.

David Lloyd: "Moonlit" from HM 4/4, copyright © 1970 by Eric W. Amann; "At the bottom" from HW 6/2, copyright © 1973 by Leroy Kanterman; "The longest" from FR II/1, © 1979 HSA, "Quietly" from NWH 1/1, copyright © 1973 The Heliopolis Press: all other poems (3) from *The Circle*, Charles E. Tuttle, copyright © 1974 by David Lloyd; by permission of the author.

Joanne Morcom: "surrounding" from *RAW NerVZ* III/1, copyright © 1996 by Joanne Morcom; by permission of the author.

Marlene Mountain: "winter" from MH XVII/1, copyright © 1986 by Marlene Mountain; "wood" from MH VII/4, copyright © 1976 by Kay Titus Mormino; "pig" from FR II/3-4, copyright © 1979 HSA; "empty" and "a quiet" from CI 1/2, © CI 1977; "he leans" from *Amoskeag* 1, copyright © 1980 by The First Haiku Press; "on this" from *moment/moment moments*, HCP, © 1978 Marlene Wills; "early" from WC 8, copyright © 1986 by Hal Roth; "old towel" from CI 1/4, © CI 1977; "pick-up" from FR III/2, copyright © 1980 HSA; "one fly" from CI 2/1, © CI 1978; "summer" from *Uguisu* 2, copyright © 1977 by Matsuo-Allard; "above" from WC 19, copyright © 1986 by Hal Roth; "faded" from WC 8, copyright © 1983 by Hal Roth; "seed" from FR III/1, copyright © 1980 HSA; "acid" and "old pond" from *pissed off poems and cross words,* copyright © 1986 by Marlene Mountain; all other poems (5) from *the old tin roof*, copyright Marlene Wills 1976; by permission of the author.

Patricia Neubauer: "first" from MH XXII/2, copyright © 1991 by Patricia Neubauer; "toy" from WN 27, copyright © 1995 by Patricia Neubauer; "winter" from WN 16, copyright © 1993 by Patricia Neubauer; "neighbor's" from MH XX/1, copyright © 1989 by Patricia Neubauer; "evening" from FR XVIII/1, copyright © 1995 by Patricia Neubauer; "moonless" from MH XXI/3, copyright © 1990 by Patricia Neubauer; by

(18) from *Hike*, copyright © 1984 by Alan Pizzarelli; by permission of the author.

Jane Reichhold: "putting" from MH XVI/3, copyright © 1985 by Jane Reichhold; all other poems (3) from *Tigers in a Cup of Tea*, AHA Books, copyright © 1988 by Jane Reichhold; by permission of the author.

Raymond Roseliep: "unable" from *Step on the Rain*, The Rook Press, copyright © 1977 by Raymond Roseliep, © renewed 1983, Daniel J. Rogers; "piano" from *Virtual Image* 1/1, copyright © W. Elliot Grieg 1982; "buttoning," "downpour," "seance," and "snow" from *Rabbit in the Moon*, Alembic Press, copyright © 1983 by Raymond Roseliep, © renewed 1985, Daniel J. Rogers; "in white tulips," "flea," and "swish" from *Swish of Cow Tail*, Swamp Press, copyright © 1982 by Raymond Roseliep, © renewed 1983, Daniel J. Rogers; "the cat" from HC 2/8, © 1978 Randy & Shirley Brooks; "after Beethoven," "in the stream," "leaving," "by the autumn hill," and "he removes" from *Sailing Bones*, The Rook Press, Ruffsdale, PA, copyright © 1978 by Raymond Roseliep, © renewed 1983, Daniel J. Rogers; "tape" from *The Still Point*, Uzzano 16, © 1979 by Raymond Roseliep, © renewed 1983, Daniel J. Rogers; all other poems (8) from *Listen to Light*, Alembic Press, Plainfield, IN, copyright © 1980 by Raymond Roseliep, © renewed 1983, Daniel J. Rogers; by permission of The Rev. Daniel J. Rogers.

Bruce Ross: "morning train" from WN 22, copyright © 1994 by Bruce Ross; "Thoreau's" from MH XXV/3, copyright © 1994 by Bruce Ross; "sunny" from MH

Rotella; all other poems (13) from *On a White Bud*, Merging Media, copyright © 1983 by Alexis Rotella; by permission of the author.

Martin Shea: "warehouse" from *Tweed* 4/3, copyright © 1976 by Janice M. Bostok; "red-flashing" from NWH 1/2, copyright © 1973 The Heliopolis Press; "the long night" from MH IV/3, copyright © 1973 by Kay Titus Mormino; "walk's end" and "sparrows" from *across the loud stream*, SOP, copyright © 1974 by Martin Shea; "bolted" from NWH 1/3, copyright © 1974 The Heliopolis Press; "Moving" from HM 6/1-2, © William J. Higginson 1974; "terminal" from SO 3, copyright © 1975 by Michael McClintock; "held it" from *blackdog in the headlights*, Shelters Press, copyright © 1975 by Martin Shea; "winter" previously unpublished; by permission of the author.

George Skane: "warm spring day" from FR XV/1, copyright © 1992 by George Skane; by permission of the author.

Karen Sohne: "driving" and "no moon" from FR XIV/1, copyright © 1991 by Karen Sohne; "between" and "after lights" from *After Lights Out*, SS, copyright © 1996 by Karen Sohne; "ever since" from *rain so loud*, proof press, copyright © 1994 by Karen Sohne; "the men," "stocking," and "the haiku" from *A Small Umbrella*, SS, copyright © 1995 by Karen Sohne; "androgynous" and "horror" from *Woodshavings*, SS, copyright © 1994 by Karen Sohne; by permission of the author.

O. Mabson Southard: "Mirrored" from HW 6/2, copyright © 1973 by Leroy Kanterman; "Perching" and "Hushed"

Swede; "A sigh" from FR XX/2, © 1997 George Swede; "Swinging," "Unhappy," "One by one," and "On the face" from *All of Her Shadows*, HCP, © 1982 George Swede; "Night," "One button," and "Summer" from *Wingbeats*, Juniper Press, © 1979 George Swede; "On the bus" from *Endless Jigsaw*, © 1978 George Swede; "stars" from CI 5/3, © CI 1978; "in the town" from *Amoskeag* 1, copyright © 1980 by The First Haiku Press; "At dawn" from CI 3/3, © CI 1979; "Windless" and "At the edge" from *A Snowman, Headless*, Fiddlehead, copyright © 1979 by George Swede; "Long" from MH XXIV/3, © 1993 George Swede; "Mental" and "After" from *Eye to Eye with a Frog*, Juniper Press, copyright 1981 by George Swede; "Passport" from CI 2/4, © CI 1978; "Thick" from FR XX/2, © 1997 George Swede; all other poems (6) from *Leaving My Loneliness*, KR, copyright © 1992 by George Swede; by permission of the author.

Wally Swist: "dewy," "trembling," "tugging," "walking," and "a white mare" from *The Mown Meadow*, Los Hombres Press, © 1996 by Wally Swist; "thunder" from MH XXV/1, © 1994 Wally Swist; "row" from MH XVII/3, © 1986 Wally Swist; "windy" from MH XXIX/1, © 1998 Wally Swist; all other poems (5) from *Blowing Reeds*, Timberline Press, Fulton, MO, © 1995 by Wally Swist; by permission of the author.

Tom Tico: "Sitting" from WN 25, © 1995 by Tom Tico; all other poems (4) from *Spring Morning Sun*, Morris Publishing, © 1998 by Tom Tico; by permission of the author.

bird" from MH XXIV/1, © 1993 by Michael Dylan Welch; "mountain" from FR XIII/2, © 1990 by Michael Dylan Welch; "beach" from FR XXI/2, © 1998 by Michael Dylan Welch; "low" from *The Shortest Distance*, HNA Anthology, © 1993 by Michael Dylan Welch; "after the quake / adding" from *Mirrors* III/1, © 1990 by Michael Dylan Welch; "fresh snow" from FR XV/2, © 1992 by Michael Dylan Welch; "after dinner" from *When Butterflies Come*, HSA Anthology, © 1993 by Michael Dylan Welch; "toll booth" from FR XVIII/4, © 1995 Michael Dylan Welch; "spring breeze—" from WN 19, © 1993 by Michael Dylan Welch; "my face" from MH XXII/1, © 1991 by Michael Dylan Welch; "after the quake / the" from FR XIII/1, © 1990 by Michael Dylan Welch; "first day" and "grocery" from *Fig Newtons: Senryu to Go*, Press Here, Foster City, CA, © 1993 by Michael Dylan Welch; "reading" from *Hummingbird* VII/2, © 1996 by Michael Dylan Welch; "first snow" from WN 23, © 1994 by Michael Dylan Welch; "taking" from WN 29, © 1996 by Michael Dylan Welch; "paper" from MH XXVI/3, © 1995 by Michael Dylan Welch; "home" from *Ko* (Aut-Wtr 1995), © 1995 by Michael Dylan Welch; by permission of the author.

Larry Wiggin: "scouring" and "fly" from *loose kites*, copyright © 1973 Larry Wiggin: "dreaming" and "wind" from *The Haiku Anthology* (1st edition), © 1974 Cor van den Heuvel; "crickets" from HM 5/2, © William J. Higginson 1971; by permission of David Wiggins.

Rod Willmot: "first morning" from HM 2/1, © 1968 by

River, copyright © 1978 by Virginia Brady Young; all other poems (4) from *Circle of Thaw*, Barlenmir House, copyright © 1972 by Virginia Brady Young; by permission of the author.

Arizona Zipper: "Right" from FR VI/2, © 1983 HSA; "Opening" and "In the shade" from *Selections From A Pale Leaf*, copyright © 1991 by Arizona Zipper; "After," "Hopping," and "I stop" from *A Pale Leaf*, copyright © 1981 by Arizona Zipper; "Following" from FR VII/4, © 1984 HSA; "Hard climb" from post card, copyright © 1985 by Arizona Zipper; all other poems (11) from *Fryeburg Fair*, copyright © 1987 by Arizona Zipper; by permission of the author.